SOS ITALIAN GRAMMAR A1-A2

A Simplified Italian grammar for everyone

By Chiara Brambilla

Copyright © 2018 by Chiara Brambilla

All rights reserved. No part of this publication may be reproduced in any form or by any means, including scanning, photocopying, or otherwise without prior written permission of the copyright holder.

TABLE OF CONTENTS

Introduction .... **XIII**

Chapter 1 - The alphabet **1**
   1.1 - Vowels 2
   1.2 - Consonants 4
   1.3 - Other consonant sounds 9
   1.4 - Double consonants 13
   1.5 - Tonic accent 14

Chapter 2 - The italian sentence **16**
   2.1 - The interrogative sentence – formation 17

Chapter 3 - The noun **19**
   3.1 - Masculine nouns 20
   3.2 - Feminine nouns 20
   3.3 - Masculine or feminine? 21
   3.4 - Changing nouns from masculine to feminine 22
   3.5 - The plural of nouns 24
      3.5.1 - Masculine nouns ending in -cio and -gio 27

3.5.2 - Feminine nouns ending in -cia and -gia 27
3.6 - Compound nouns 29
 3.6.1 - Noun + noun 29
 3.6.2 - Adjective + adjective 30
 3.6.3 - Noun + adjective; adjective + noun 31
 3.6.4 - Verb + verb 31
 3.6.5 - Verb + noun; noun + verb 32
 3.6.6 - Adverb + verb; verb + adverb 33
 3.6.7 - Adverb + adjective 33
 3.6.8 - Preposition + noun; adverb + noun 34
3.7 - Altered nouns 35
 3.7.1 - Diminutive suffixes 35
  3.7.1.1 - Other uses of diminutives 37
 3.7.2 - Augmentative suffixes 38
 3.7.3 - Endearing suffixes 39
 3.7.4 - Pejorative suffixes 40

Chapter 4 - The verb 42

4.1 - Auxiliaries 42
 4.1.1 - Avere 43
 4.1.2 - Essere 45
  4.1.2.1 – Difference between the verb essere and the verb stare
  46
4.2 - The present tense 53

- 4.2.1 - The present tense of regular verbs 55
- 4.2.2 - The present tense of irregular verbs 61
- 4.3 - Reflexive verbs 64
- 4.4 - Modal verbs 66
  - 4.4.1 - Potere 68
  - 4.4.2 - Dovere 68
  - 4.4.3 - Volere 69
  - 4.4.4 - Sapere 70
  - 4.4.5 - Difference between sapere and potere as modal verbs .. 71
  - 4.4.6 - Modal verbs and atonic pronouns 72
  - 4.4.7 - Modal verbs with compound tenses 73
- 4.5 - The imperative 76
  - 4.5.1 - Formation of regular verbs 77
  - 4.5.2 - Formation of irregular verbs 79
  - 4.5.3 - The imperative and tonic and atonic personal pronouns 81
- 4.6 - The past participle 82
  - 4.6.1 - Position and agreement 84
  - 4.6.2 – Formation of regular verbs 85
  - 4.6.3 – Formation of irregular verbs 85
- 4.7 - Passato prossimo 86
  - 4.7.1 - Formation 87
  - 4.7.2 - Passato prossimo and atonic personal pronouns 92
  - 4.7.3 - Passato prossimo and reflexive verbs 93
- 4.8 – The imperfetto 94
  - 4.8.1 – Formation of regular verbs 96

4.8.2 – Formation of irregular verbs 97

4.9 - Difference between imperfetto and passato prossimo 99

4.10 - How to talk about actions that happened at the same time in the past 102

4.11 – Phraseological verbs..103

4.12 - The simple future 107

    4.12.1 – Formation of regular verbs 109

    4.12.2 – Formation of irregular verbs..................................110

    4.12.3 - Verbs ending in -care, -gare 115

    4.12.4 - Verbs ending in -ciare, -giare 116

4.13 - The present conditional...117

    4.13.1 – Formation of regular verbs 119

    4.13.2 – Formation of irregular verbs..................................121

    4.13.3 - Verbs ending in -care, -gare 124

    4.13.4 - Verbs ending in -ciare, -giare 125

Chapter 5 - The articles 127

5.1 - Definite articles..127

    5.1.1 - Feminine singular...128

    5.1.2 - Masculine singular 128

    5.1.3 - Feminine plural 129

    5.1.4 - Masculine plural..129

    5.1.5 - Use 130

5.2 - Indefinite articles 132

5.2.1 - Feminine indefinite articles 133
5.2.2 - Masculine indefinite articles 133
5.3 - Partitive articles 134
   5.3.1 - Singular partitive articles 134
      5.3.1.1 - Masculine partitive articles 135
      5.3.1.2 - Feminine partitive articles 136
   5.3.2 - Plural partitive articles 137
      5.3.2.1 - Masculine partitive articles 137
      5.3.2.2 - Feminine partitive articles 138
   5.3.3 - When partitive articles are not used 140

Chapter 6 - Numbers 141

6.1 - Cardinal numbers 141
   6.1.1 - Numbers from 0 to 10 141
   6.1.2 - Numbers from 11 to 19 142
   6.1.3 – Tens 143
   6.1.4 - How to form and read numbers 143
   6.1.5 – Hundreds 145
   6.1.6 – Thousands 146
   6.1.7 - How to read years 147
   6.1.8 - Agreement of cardinal numbers 147
6.2 - Ordinal numbers 148
   6.2.1 - How to form and read ordinal numbers 149
   6.2.2 - How to read centuries 150

6.2.3 - Agreement of ordinal numbers 150

Chapter 7 - Adjectives 152

7.1 - Feminine and masculine of adjectives 152

7.1.1 - Adjectives ending in -o 152

7.1.2 - Adjectives ending in -e 153

7.1.3 - Adjectives ending in -a 153

7.2 - Plural of adjectives 154

7.2.1 - Adjectives ending in –o 154

7.2.1.1 - Adjectives ending in -cio and -gio 155

7.2.2 - Adjectives ending in -e 156

7.2.3 - Adjectives ending in -a 157

7.2.4 - Other information 157

7.3 - Interrogative adjectives 158

7.3.1 - Quantity 158

7.3.2 - Quality or identity 159

7.4 - Demonstrative adjectives 160

7.4.1 - Near objects 160

7.4.2 - Distant objects 162

7.4.3 - Recap 164

7.5 - Possessive adjectives 165

7.6 - Indefinite adjectives 169

7.6.1 - Alcuno, certo, vario, diverso 169

7.6.2 - Altro 170

7.6.3 - Molto 171
7.6.4 - Nessuno 171
7.6.5 - Ogni 172
7.6.6 - Parecchio 172
7.6.7 - Poco 173
7.6.8 - Qualche 173
7.6.9 - Qualsiasi 174
7.6.10 - Qualunque 174
7.6.11 - Tale 175
7.6.12 - Tanto 175
7.6.13 - Troppo 175
7.6.14 - Tutto 176

Chapter 8 - Pronouns 177

8.1 - Personal subject pronouns 177
   8.1.1 - Personal subject pronouns - the courtesy form 180
8.2 - Personal object pronouns 181
   8.2.1 - Tonic personal pronouns replacing direct objects 182
   8.2.2 - Tonic personal pronouns replacing indirect objects 183
   8.2.3 - Atonic personal pronouns replacing direct objects 185
   8.2.4 - Atonic personal pronouns replacing indirect objects ... 186
8.3 - Possessive pronouns 187
8.4 - Interrogative pronouns 190
   8.4.1 - Chi 190

8.4.2 - Che/che cosa/cosa 190

8.4.3 - Quale/i – qual 191

8.4.4 - Quanto/a/i/e 192

8.5 - Indefinite pronouns 192

8.5.1 - Alcuno, certo 192

8.5.2 - Altro 193

8.5.3 - Chiunque 193

8.5.4 - Ciascuno, ognuno 193

8.5.5 - Molto 194

8.5.6 - Nessuno 194

8.5.7 - Niente 194

8.5.8 - Nulla 195

8.5.9 - Parecchio 195

8.5.10 - Poco 195

8.5.11 - Qualcosa 196

8.5.12 - Qualcuno 196

8.5.13 - Tanto 196

8.5.14 - Troppo 197

8.5.15 - Tutto 197

8.5.16 - Uno 198

8.5.17 - Vario, diverso 198

Chapter 9 - Adverbs 199

9.1 - Formation 199

9.2 - Types of adverbs in italian 200

    9.2.1 - Adverbs of manner 201

    9.2.2 - Adverbs of place 202

    9.2.3 - Adverbs of time 202

    9.2.4 - Adverbs of degree 203

    9.2.5 - Adverbs of quantity 204

    9.2.6 - Interrogative adverbs 205

9.3 - The position of adverbs 207

Chapter 10 - Prepositions 210

10.1 - Simple prepositions 210

    10.1.1 - Di 211

    10.1.2 - A 213

    10.1.3 - Da 214

    10.1.4 - In 216

    10.1.5 - Con 217

    10.1.6 - Su 218

    10.1.7 - Per 218

    10.1.8 - Tra/fra 220

10.2 - Contracted prepositions 221

    10.2.1 - Con 224

    10.2.2 - Su 224

10.3 - Simple prepositions or contracted prepositions? 225

Chapter 11 - Conjunctions 230

11.1 - Coordinating conjunctions 231

11.2 - Subordinating conjunctions 237

Chapter 12 - There is and there are 247

12.1 - Other meanings of c'e' and ci sono 248

Chapter 13 - The comparative and the superlative 250

13.1 - The comparative 250

   13.1.1 - Expressing superiority 251

   13.1.2 - Expressing inferiority 252

   13.1.3 - Expressing equality 253

   13.1.4 - Irregular comparative forms 254

13.2 - The superlative 256

   13.2.1 - Relative superlative 256

      13.2.1.1 - Expressing the highest degree of a quality 256

      13.2.1.2 - Expressing the least degree of a quality 257

   13.2.2 - Absolute superlative 258

      13.2.2.1 - Expressing the highest degree of a quality 258

   13.2.3 - Other ways to form absolute superlative 259

   13.2.4 - Irregular superlative forms 260

Chapter 14 - The impersonal form 262

14.1 – The impersonal form with si 265

Chapter 15 - Conditional clauses 268

15.1 – Conditional clauses expressing certainty 269

Glossary 272

Contacts 2724

*** If you want to test your knowledge and understanding of Italian grammar for levels A1-A2, sign up to my mailing list and get a free pdf with some Italian grammar exercises - https://www.italiantranslation-teaching.com/free-italian-grammar-exercises/ ***

Introduction

Welcome to Sos Italian grammar A1-A2.

This grammar has been developed to help you grasp the basics of the Italian grammar.

It includes all the main topics that are studied at levels A1 and A2. For this reason, it can also be a valid aid to recap all the grammatical topics you need to master to pass the grammatical part of the exam to get the Italian certifications Cils and Celi.

I know very well that grammar can sometimes be a little bit difficult to understand and master, so when I wrote this grammar I tried to keep it as simple as possible while making it precise and complete for A1 A2 levels.

To make it as simple as possible, I tried to avoid the use of technical terms. The only few technical terms you'll find are the ones that have entered common language such as noun, verb, adverb, conjunction, etc. However, even in this case, these terms are clearly explained both in each dedicated chapter and in a glossary at the end of this grammar.

Now, a few words about the structure of this grammar.

The table of contents is organized by topic – i.e. under the chapter on verbs all of the verb tenses addressed will be listed; under the chapter on adjectives all of the types of adjectives addressed will be listed; etc.

The grammar is divided into chapters, each dealing with a specific grammatical topic. In each chapter there are clear explanations and examples. Each example comes also with its English translation to ease comprehension.

I hope you'll find this book a useful and easy guide to Elementary Italian grammar.

PS: If you want to deepen your knowledge of Italian and Italian culture, you might find the blog section of my website interesting – Sositalian.com

PPS: If you want to test your knowledge and understanding of Italian grammar for levels A1-A2, sign up to my mailing list and get a free pdf with some Italian grammar exercises - https://www.italiantranslation-teaching.com/free-italian-grammar-exercises/

Chapter 1
The alphabet

In Italian each letter has a specific sound. Sometimes, a combination of two or more letters has a specific sound. If you learn these sounds, you will be able to read every Italian word you encounter.

The Italian alphabet is generally composed of 21 letters because j, k, w, x, and y aren't generally used. However, you can still encounter some of these letters in some Italian words, especially those of foreign origin.

Below we will study letter by letter. Below each letter, you will find the IPA (International Phonetic Alphabet) pronunciation of an Italian word first. Then you will find the Italian word, followed by its English translation.

In the English translation, you will see that one or more letters are underlined. These underlined letters are the ones that have a similar sound to the Italian letter we are focusing on.

For example, the letter "a" in Italian has a very similar sound to the letter "u" in c<u>u</u>p.

If you want to hear how the Italian words written below are pronounced in Italian, type them on this online free dictionary, Dizionario italiano - http://www.dizionario-italiano.it.

1.1 - Vowels

In Italian there are five vowels: a, i, u, e, o.

A

/'tattsa/ -> Tazza -> C<u>u</u>p

/'makkina/ -> Macchina -> C<u>a</u>r

I

/i'djɔta/ -> Idiota -> <u>I</u>d<u>i</u>ot

/i'dea/ -> Idea -> id<u>e</u>a

U

/'kwɔko/ -> Cuoco -> C<u>oo</u>k

/'uno/ -> Uno -> <u>o</u>ne

E………s<u>e</u>t (open sound), t<u>a</u>ke (closed sound)

In Italian the vowel "e" can have either an open sound or a closed one. The open sound is similar to the sound of the letter "e" in *set*.

/pɛska'notʃe/ -> P<u>e</u>scanoce -> n<u>e</u>ctarine (open)
/ vjo'let:a/ -> Violetta -> viol<u>e</u>t (open)

The closed sound is a little bit more complex to explain without hearing the sound in real time. Let's say that it is similar to half of the sound the letter "a" has in the word *take* /te<u>ɪ</u>k/.

/'vetro/ -> Vetro (closed)
/'venti/ -> Venti (closed)

O

In Italian the vowel "o" can have either an open sound or a closed one. The open sound is similar to the sound of the letter "o" in *octagon*.

/'ɔljo/ -> <u>O</u>lio -> <u>o</u>il (open)

On the other hand, the closed sound is similar to the sound of the letter "o" in *snow* /sn<u>oʊ</u>/.

/'kome/ -> Come (closed)
/'kome/ -> Colosseo (closed)

1.2 - Consonants

The main 16 consonants used in Italian are: b, c, d, f, g, h, l, m, n, p, q, r, s, t, v, z.

If you have difficulties with the sounds below, remember to check how the Italian words are pronounced by using the free online dictionary Dizionario Italiano.

B (bi)

/baˈnana/ -> Banana -> banana

/kaˈbina/ -> Cabina -> cabin

C (ci)

/karˈrɛllo/ -> Carrello -> kart

/kaˈrino/ -> Carino -> cute

D (di)

/desˈtino/ -> Destino -> destiny

/ˈdado/ -> Dado -> dice

F (effe)

/ˈfjore/ -> Fiore -> flower

/foˈrɛsta/ -> Foresta -> forest

G (gi)

/ˈgas/ -> Gas -> gas

/ˈgamba/ -> Gamba -> leg

H (acca)

The letter "h" in Italian has no sound. So when pronouncing a word that starts with h, Italians simply start pronouncing it from the letter that comes immediately after.

/oˈtɛl/ -> Hotel

/ˈabitat/ -> Habitat

L (elle)

/ˈlungo/ -> Lungo > long

/leˈtsjone/ -> Lezione -> lesson

M (emme)

/ˈmamma/ -> Mamma -> mom

/monˈtaɲa/ -> Montagna -> mountain

N (enne)

/ˈnɔnno/ -> Nonno -> grandfather

/ˈnɔtte/ -> Notte -> night

P (pi)

/perˈsona/ -> Persona -> person

/ˈpera/ -> Pera -> pear

Q (cu)

/kwoˈtsjɛnte/ Quoziente -> quotient

R (erre)

/riˈpɔso/ -> Riposo -> rest

/reliˈdʒone/ -> Religione -> religion

S (esse)

/ˈsanto/ -> Santo -> saint

/ˈsimile/ -> Simile -> similar

T (ti)

/ˈtavolo/ -> Tavolo -> table

/ˈte/ -> Tè -> tea

V (vi)

/ˈvjɔla/ -> Viola -> violet

/ˈvizita/ -> Visita -> visit

Z (zeta)

Z can have two sounds in Italian. The first sound can be similar to the sound of the letters "ds" in *lads*.

/dzan'dzara/ -> Zanzara

The second sound can be similar to the sound of the letters "ts" in *cats*.

/'tsukkero/ -> Zucchero

Although there are rules in phonetics about when to use these two sounds, I am not going to list them here. The great majority of Italians usually do not follow them, choosing to use the first or the second sound generally according to the Italian region they belong to.

J (jay or i lunga)

The letter "j" in Italian can be pronounced as the Italian vowel "i."

/'jakopo/ -> Jacopo -> Jacopo

However, with words borrowed from another language (i.e. as French or English), the letter "j" is pronounced as it is pronounced in the language where the word was borrowed.

/ˈdʒins/ -> Jeans -> Jeans

/abaˈʒur/ -> Abat-jour -> Abat-jour

K (cappa)

The letter "k" in Italian has the same sound as in English.

/ˈkarma/ -> Karma -> Karma

W (vu doppia)

The letter "w" in Italian is generally pronounced as the letter "v."

/ˈvurstel/ -> Würstel (Vienna sausage)

/ˈvater/ -> Water (WC)

However, with words borrowed from English, the letter "w" is pronounced most of the time as it is pronounced in English

/ˈwɛb/ -> Web -> Web

X (ics)

The letter "x" in Italian has the same sound as in English.

/kseˈnɔfobo/ -> Xenofobo -> Xenophobe

Y (ipsilon or i greca)

Finally, the letter "y" in Italian is generally pronounced as the same letter in English.

/ˈbɛbi/ -> Baby -> Baby
/bajˈpas/ -> Bypass -> Bypass

1.3 - Other consonant sounds

In Italian when some letters combine, they acquire a whole new sound.

If you have difficulties with the sounds below, remember to check how the Italian words are pronounced by going to the free online dictionary Dizionario Italiano.

C + E or C + I

When "c" is followed by "e" or "i," this combination acquires the same sound as the letters "cha" in *chain* and "chi" in *chin*.

Chain – Chin

/ˈtʃena/ -> Cena (dinner)
/ˈtʃinema/ -> Cinema (cinema)

G + E or G + I

Similarly, when "g" is followed by "e" or "i," this combination acquires the same sound as the letters "ja" in *jam* and "gi" in *gin*.

<u>J</u>am – <u>J</u>in

/ˈdʒɛnte/ -> <u>G</u>ente (people)
/ˈdʒita/ -> <u>G</u>ita (trip)

CHE or CHI

When "c" is followed by "he" or "hi," this combination acquires the same sound as the letters "ca" in *can* and "ki" in *kilt*.

<u>C</u>an – <u>K</u>ilt

/ˈmoske/ -> Mos<u>che</u> (flies)
/ˈɛki/ -> E<u>chi</u> (echoes)

GHE or GHI

Similarly, when "g" is followed by "he" or "hi," this combination acquires the same sound as the letters "gue" in *guest* and "gui" in *guilt*.

<u>Gue</u>st – <u>Gui</u>lt

/ˈrige/ -> Ri<u>gh</u>e (lines)

/ˈgiro/ -> <u>Ghi</u>ro (dormouse)

SC + E or SC + I

When "sc" is followed by "e" or "i," this combination acquires the same sound as the letters "she" in *shell* and "shi" in *ship*.

<u>Sh</u>ell – <u>Sh</u>ip

/ˈpeʃʃe/ -> Pe<u>sce</u> (fish)

/ˈeʃʃi/ -> E<u>sci</u> (go out)

GN

The most similar sound to "gn" in English is a borrowing from Spanish. Think about how the letter "ñ" is pronounced in El Niño and transfer the same sound to the Italian combination "gn."

/ˈsoɲɲo/ -> Sogno (dream)

/ˈreɲɲi/ -> Regni (Realms)

GL + I

The sound "gli" is often considered one of the most difficult to learn. However, here is a little trick that is usually considered useful by the majority of learners.

First, listen to the pronunciation of a word that has the sound "gli" by checking the free online dictionary Dizionario Italiano.

Then, try to pronounce the sound "gli" in that word as if you were trying to pronounce the double "l." You'll see that with some practice you should be able to pronounce the Italian sound "gli" without problems.

/ˈfiʎʎo/ -> Figlio (child)
/ˈfɔʎʎa/ -> Foglia (leaf)

If despite all your efforts you still have problems pronouncing the "gli" sound, you will probably be relieved to know that some Italians pronounce it as the sound "y" in *yield*.

Yield

/ˈfijo/ -> Figlio
/ˈfɔja/ -> Foglia

ATTENZIONE - ATTENTION
GLI + Consonant………glisten

Pay attention because when the "gli" is followed by a consonant, its pronunciation changes. In fact, in this case, you should pronounce its letters separately, as the sound "gli" in *glisten* and in *glimpse*.

Glisten – Glimpse

/ˈglitʃine/ -> Glicine (wisteria)
/glitʃeˈmia/ -> Glicemia (glycemia)

1.4 - Double consonants

In Italian there are also double consonants. These consonants usually have the same pronounciation as the single ones, but you will have to pronounce them a bit stronger.

It is very important to pronounce double consonants correctly because they can make the difference between two different words.

For example, *caro* means "dear" but *carro* means "cart."

As usual, my advice is to check how the Italian words below are pronounced by checking the free online dictionary Dizionario Italiano so you can hear the difference between double consonants and single consonants.

Farro (hulled wheat) – Faro (light house)

Colla (glue) – Cola (it pours)

Cassa (box) – Casa (house)

Coppia (couple) – Copia (copy)

Nonno (grandfather) – Nono (ninth)

1.5 - Tonic accent

The best thing you can do to learn Italian tonic accent is to listen to native speakers, podcasts, movies, radio, etc.

When pronouncing a word, we tend to give some relative phonetic prominence to a specific syllable of that word. This prominence we give is called tonic accent.

For example, in the English word <u>in</u>dustry the tonic accent is on the first syllable. On the other hand, in the English word in<u>du</u>strial, the tonic accent is on the second syllable.

According to the position of the tonic accent, words can be tronche, piane, sdrucciole, or bisdrucciole.

- Words that are tronche have a tonic accent on their last syllable – pap<u>à</u>, per<u>ò</u>, etc.

- Words that are piane have a tonic accent on their second last syllable – p<u>a</u>ne, gior<u>na</u>le, etc.
- Words that are sdrucciole have a tonic accent on their third last syllable – t<u>a</u>volo, ve<u>ri</u>fica, etc.
- Words that are bisdrucciole have a tonic accent on their fourth last syllable – ve<u>ri</u>ficano, <u>a</u>bitano, etc.

SOME RULES ON THE POSITION OF THE TONIC ACCENT

Generally, there aren't rules that can help you understand where to place the tonic accent in Italian.

However, there are at least three rules concerning Italian words that are sdrucciole.

1. In Italian nouns ending in -agine, -aggine, -igine, -iggine, -edine, -udine are usually sdruccioli.
2. In Italian nouns and adjectives ending in -abile, -ibile, -evole, -aceo, -ico, -ognolo, -oide are usually sdruccioli.
3. In Italian compound words ending in -cefalo, -crate, -crono, -dromo, -fago, -filo, -fobo, -fono, -geno, -grafo, -logo, -mano, -metro, -ttero are usually sdrucciole.

Chapter 2

The italian sentence

In general Italian has a SVO structure: subject + verb + object + other elements.

Ex: Maria (subject) mangia (verb) una mela (object)

Maria (subject) eats (verb) an apple (object)

However, in Italian sentences don't necessarily have a fixed structure.

For example, some adverbs can be placed in different positions:

Ex1: Ultimamente Maria mangia poco

Lately, Maria doesn't eat a lot

Ex2: Maria mangia poco ultimamente

Lately, Maria doesn't eat a lot

Ex3: Maria ultimamente mangia poco

Lately, Maria doesn't eat a lot

2.1 - The interrogative sentence – formation

To form interrogative sentences in Italian, you add a question mark at the end of the sentence.

Examples:

Statement: E' arrivato il pacco che aspettavo
　　　　　The package I was waiting for has arrived

Question: E' arrivato il pacco che aspettavo?
　　　　　Has the package I was waiting for arrived?

When pronouncing questions, remember to raise the pitch at the end of the question.

Examples:

Statement: E' arrivato il pacco che aspettavo

──────────────▶

Question: E' arrivato il pacco che aspettavo?

──────────────▶

2.2 - The negative sentence – formation

To form negative sentences in Italian, you just add the word *non* before the verb.

Examples:

Affirmative sentence: Io ho fame
                     I'm hungry

Negative sentence: Io <u>non</u> ho fame
                     I'm not hungry

Chapter 3

The noun

A noun denotes an entity or a concept.

In Italian, nouns are generally used with articles, and they can be masculine, feminine, or both.

How can we recognize them?

Although it's not always easy to spot masculine and feminine nouns in Italian, there are some rules that can help you.

In Italian singular nouns can end in -o, -a, -e, or -i

3.1 - Masculine nouns

The majority of nouns ending in -o is generally masculine:

Ex: Uov**o** -> Egg (masculine)

Some Exceptions

Auto -> car (feminine)

Radio -> radio (feminine)

Eco -> echo (feminine)

3.2 - Feminine nouns

A lot of nouns ending in -a are generally feminine:

Example: Mel**a** -> Apple (feminine)

Some exceptions

Clima -> climate (masculine)

Enigma -> enigma/riddle (masculine)

Asma -> asthma (masculine)

Nouns ending in -tà are feminine:

Ex: Cit**tà** -> City (feminine)

Most of Italian nouns ending in -**i** or -**ù** are feminine:

Ex: Cris**i** -> Crisis/attack (feminine)
Ex: Virt**ù**-> Virtue (feminine)

Exceptions

Cucù -> cuckoo clock (masculine)
Tutù -> tutu (masculine)

3.3 - Masculine or feminine?

Nouns ending in -e and in -i can be either masculine or feminine. Unfortunately, there isn't a rule to know if a noun ending in -e or in -i is masculine or feminine. One possible solution is to look a noun up in a dictionary.

FEMININE	**MASCULINE**
Televisione (television)	Errore (error/mistake)
Chiave (key)	Cane (dog)
Analisi (analysis)	Sci (ski)
Ipotesi (hypothesis)	Lunedì (Monday)

3.4 - Changing nouns from masculine to feminine

Some nouns, generally those referring to human beings and animals, have both a masculine and a feminine form, depending if the subject they're referring to is a male or a female.

To change nouns from masculine to feminine, you generally replace the final letter -o, with the vowel -a.

Examples:
>Ragazzo (boy) -> Ragazza (girl)
>Amico (male friend) -> Amica (Female friend)
>Zio (uncle) -> Zia (Aunt)

However, sometimes masculine and feminine nouns, referring to human beings and animals, have two completely different forms.

Examples:
>Uomo (Man) -> Donna (Woman)
>Gallo (Cock) -> Gallina (Chicken)

NOUNS THAT CAN BE BOTH MASCULINE AND FEMININE

In Italian some nouns can be both masculine and feminine.

Some examples are:

L'Agente -> policeman/agent
Il/la Cantante -> singer
Il/la Nipote -> grandchild/nephew/niece
Il/la Custode -> keeper/warden/concierge/guard
Il/la Negoziante -> storekeeper
Il/la Parente -> relative

NOUNS REFERRING TO A PROFESSION

Let's see how to change masculine nouns into feminine nouns when they refer to a profession.

Masculine nouns ending in -e

Nouns ending in -e may form the feminine either replacing the final **-e** with **-a** or with **-essa**.

- Cameriere (Waiter) -> Camerier**a** (Waitress)
- Infermiere (Male nurse) -> Infermier**a** (Female nurse)
- Studente (Male student) -> Student**essa** (Female student)

Masculine nouns ending in -tore

Nouns ending in **-tore** may form the feminine form replacing **-tore** with **-trice**.

- At**tore** (Actor) -> At**trice** (Actress)
- Scul**tore** (Male sculptor) -> Scul**trice** (Female sculptor)

3.5 - The plural of nouns

Let's see how to form the plural of nouns in Italian.

NOUNS ENDING IN -A

If the nouns ending in -a are *masculine*, they change the final **-a** into **-i**:

Ex: L'enigma -> Gli enigmi (enigmas/riddles)

If the nouns ending in -a are *feminine*, they change the final **-a** into **-e**:

Ex: La pera -> Le pere (pears)

However, pay attention because if the feminine noun ends in -ca or -ga, it adds a "h" after "c" and "g" before it changes into the plural to preserve the hard sound of "c" and "g."

Examples:

L'oca -> le oche (geese)

L'acciuga -> le acciughe (anchovies)

La mucca -> le mucche (cows)

La valanga -> le valanghe (avalanches)

NOUNS ENDING IN -O

If the nouns ending in -o are *masculine*, they change the final -o into an -i:

Ex: Il giardino -> I giardini (gardens)

However, if the nouns ending in -o are *feminine*, in the plural they **do not change**. The only exception is **mano** (hand) which changes the final -o into an -i.

Ex: L'auto -> Le auto (car/cars)
Ex: La radio -> Le radio (radio/radios)
Ex: La mano -> Le mani (hands)

However, nouns ending in -co and -go that have a tonic accent on their second last syllable add a -h after "c" and "g" when they change into the plural. In addition, these words change the final -o into an -i when forming the plural.

Examples:

L'ago -> Gli aghi (needles)
L'eco -> Gli echi (echoes)
Il circo -> I circhi (circuses)

NOUNS ENDING IN -E

Both *masculine* and *feminine* nouns change the final **-e** into an **-i**:

Ex: La luce -> Le luci (lights - feminine)
Ex: Il dente -> I denti (teeth - masculine)

NOUNS ENDING IN -I

Both *masculine* and *feminine* nouns ending in -i do not change in the plural:

Examples:
    L'analisi -> Le analisi (analysis - feminine)
    Il brindisi -> I brindisi (toasts - masculine)

FOREIGN NOUNS

Foreign nouns do not change in the plural. The only thing to change from singular to plural is the article.

Examples:

> Il taxi -> I taxi
> L'hotel -> Gli hotel
> Lo scooter -> Gli scooter

3.5.1 - Masculine nouns ending in -cio and -gio

Nouns ending in -cio and -gio in the masculine singular form the masculine plural by deleting the final -o.

Examples:

Il mi<u>cio</u> -> I mic<u>i</u> (kitty cats)
Il segu<u>gio</u> -> I segug<u>i</u> (bloodhounds)
Il gus<u>cio</u> -> I gusc<u>i</u> (shells)
Il parche<u>ggio</u> -> I parchegg<u>i</u> (parking lots)

3.5.2 - Feminine nouns ending in -cia and -gia

Feminine nouns ending in -cia and -gia form the feminine plural in different ways.

If the syllables -cia and -gia aren't stressed and are preceded by a vowel, these feminine nouns form the plural by replacing the final -a with -e.

Examples:
L'acacia -> Le acacie (acacias)
La ciliegia -> Le ciliegie (cherries)
Le camicia -> Le camicie (blouses)
La valigia -> Le valigie (suitcases)

If the syllables -cia and -gia aren't stressed and are preceded by a consonant, these feminine nouns form the plural by replacing the final -ia with -e.

Examples:
La freccia -> Le frecce (arrows)
La spiaggia -> Le spiagge (beaches)
L'ascia -> Le asce (axes)
Torcia -> Le torce (torches)

However, if the syllables -cia and -gia are stressed, these feminine nouns form the plural by replacing the final -a with -e.

Examples:
La farmacia -> Le farmacie (drugstores)
La strategia -> Le strategie (strategies)

3.6 - Compound nouns

Compound words are those words formed by combining two or more words.

In Italian, compound words are especially common in scientific and technical terminology.
An example of a compound word used in the scientific field is gastroscopia (gastroscopy) – formed by the words gastro and scopia.

However, you can also find many compound words in standard Italian. Two examples are *maleducato* (ill-mannered) – male + educato - *mezzogiorno* (midday) – mezzo + giorno.

In Italian compound words can be formed in different ways:

3.6.1 - Noun + noun

Caffè + latte -> **Caffelatte** (latte)
Capo + classe -> **Capoclasse** (class president)
Pesce + cane -> **Pescecane** (shark)

When compound words are formed by joining together two nouns, there isn't a specific rule for the formation of the plural.

If the two nouns are of the same gender – i.e. masculine – we usually change into plural only the second noun.

Example: pesce (masculine) + cane (masculine)
pescecane -> pescecani

If the two nouns are of a different gender, we usually change into plural only the first noun.

Example: capo (masculine) + classe (feminine)
capoclasse -> capiclasse

3.6.2 - *Adjective + adjective*

Sordo + muto -> Sordomuto (deaf-mute)
Agro + dolce -> Agrodolce (sweet and sour)
Piano + forte -> Pianoforte (piano)

They form the plural by changing the suffix of the second word.

Example: pianoforte -> pianoforti

3.6.3 - Noun + adjective; adjective + noun

Mezzo + giorno -> **Mezzogiorno** (midday)

Cassa + forte -> **Cassaforte** (safe)

Basso + rilievo -> **Bassorilievo** (bas-relief)

There isn't a specific rule for the formation of the plural.

Usually, compound nouns formed by adjective + noun form the plural by changing into the plural the second word.

Example: bassorilievo -> bassorilievi

Compound nouns formed by noun + adjective, on the other hand, usually form the plural by changing into the plural both words.

Example: cassaforte -> casseforti

3.6.4 - Verb + verb

Dormi + veglia -> **Dormiveglia** (half-sleep)

Sali + scendi -> **Saliscendi** (latch)

Fuggi + fuggi -> **Fuggifuggi** (stampede)

Italian compound words formed by verb + verb do not change in the plural.

Example: dormiveglia -> **dormiveglia**

3.6.5 - *Verb + noun; noun + verb*

Porta + ombrelli -> **Portaombrelli** (umbrella stand)
Para + fango -> **Parafango** (fender)
Capo + volgere -> **Capovolgere** (to turn upside down)

Also in this case, there isn't a specific rule for the formation of the plural.

Generally, if the second word is a plural noun, the compound word does not change in the plural.

Example: portaombrelli -> **portaombrelli**

If the second word is a singular feminine noun, then the compound word, generally, does not change in the plural.

Example: spazzaneve -> **spazzaneve**

Finally, if the second word is a singular masculine noun, then only the second word changes into the plural.

Example: parafango -> parafan**ghi**

3.6.6 - Adverb + verb; verb + adverb

Mal + educato -> **Maleducato** (ill-mannered)
Male + dire -> **Maledire** (to curse)
Bene + stante -> **Benestante** (wealthy)

Italian compound words formed by adverb + verb do not change in the plural.

Example: maledire -> **maledire**

Instead, Italian compound words formed by verb + adverb generally form the plural by changing the second word into the plural.

Example: maleducato -> maleducat**i**

3.6.7 - Adverb + adjective

Sempre + verde -> **Sempreverde** (evergreen)
Mal + sano -> **Malsano** (unhealthy)

These do not change in the plural.

Example: sempreverde -> sempreverde

3.6.8 - Preposition + noun; adverb + noun

Sotto + ufficiale -> Sottufficiale (non-commissioned officer)
Lungo + mare -> Lungomare (seafront)
Inter + vista -> Intervista (interview)

If the noun used to form the compound word and the compound word are of the same gender, we form the plural by changing the noun into the plural.

Example: sottufficiale (masculine); ufficiale (masculine) -> sottufficiale -> sottufficiali

However, if the noun used to form the compound word and the compound word aren't of the same gender, the compound word remains unchanged in the plural.

Example: sottoscala (masculine); scala (feminine) -> sottoscala -> sottoscala

3.7 - Altered nouns

Altered nouns are nouns that change their meaning by adding some suffixes.

In Italian there are four types of suffixes that can be added to nouns: diminutive suffixes, augmentative suffixes, endearing suffixes, and pejorative suffixes.

3.7.1 - Diminutive suffixes

Diminutive suffixes convey an idea of smallness and agree in gender and number with the noun they are added to.

These suffixes are:

-ino

-etto

-ello

-icciolo

-(u)olo

-iciattolo

The most used diminutive suffixes in Italian are *-ino, -etto, -ello*.

Examples:

- Gattino
- Zainetto
- Alberello
- Muricciolo
- Montagnola
- Mostriciattolo

Unfortunately, there isn't a way to tell which of these suffixes is the one that has to be added to a certain noun. The only thing you can do is try to learn them.

FORMATION

These suffixes are generally added to a word after deleting its final vowel.

Ex: casa -> cas~~a~~ -> cas**etta**.

In some cases, the suffix *-ino* is preceded by *-ic* or *-ol*.

Examples:

a. Osso -> oss~~o~~ -> oss*ic* -> oss**icino**
b. Topo -> top~~o~~ -> top*ol* -> top**olino**

The suffix *-ino* can also be used in combination with the suffixes *-etto*, *-ello* and creates the suffixes *-ettino*, *-ellino*.

Examples:
a. Foglio -> foglio -> foglietto -> fogliettino
b. Storia -> storia -> storiella -> storiellina

3.7.1.1 - Other uses of diminutives

Sometimes diminutives are used to:

1. Give an order or make a request in a more gentle way

Ex: Mi faccia una firmetta qui -> Sign here, please

2. Lessen the importance, the value of something when, in reality, one is thinking the opposite

Ex: Ho comprato solo una barchetta, non è niente di che -> I just bought a little boat, nothing special.

3.7.2 - Augmentative suffixes

Augmentatives suffixes convey an idea of bigness and they usually agree in gender and number with the noun they are added to.

These suffixes are:
-one
-acchione
-accione

The most used augmentative suffix in Italian is *-one*.

Examples:
- Piede -> piede -> pied**one**
- Furbo -> furbo -> furb**acchione**
- Buono -> bon**accione**

Unfortunately, even in this case, there isn't a way to tell which of these suffixes is the one that has to be added to a certain noun. The only thing you can do is try to learn them.

3.7.3 - Endearing suffixes

Endearing suffixes convey an idea of endearment and agree in gender and number with the noun they are added to.

These suffixes are:

-ino

-etto

-uccio

-otto

-acchiotto

Many of these suffixes are the same as the diminutive ones. Thus, it will be the context that reveals if a word is used as a diminutive or as an endearment term.

Examples:
- Letto -> letto -> lettino
- Casa -> casa -> casetta
- Caldo -> caldo -> calduccio
- Lepre -> lepre -> leprotto
- Orso -> orso -> orsacchiotto

In some cases, the suffix *-ino* is preceded by *-c* or *-ic*.

Examples:

a. Balcone -> balcone -> balcon*c* -> balcon**cino**
b. Posto -> post<s>o</s> -> post*ic* -> post**icino**

Unfortunately, there isn't a way to tell which of these suffixes is the one that has to be added to a certain noun. The only thing you can do is try to learn them.

3.7.4 - Pejorative suffixes

Pejorative suffixes worsen the meaning of a word and agree in gender and number with the noun they are added to.

These suffixes are:
-accio
-astro
-uccio

The most used pejorative suffix in Italian is *-accio*.

Examples:
- Ragazzo -> ragazz<s>o</s> -> ragazz**accio**

- Ricco -> ricc~~o~~ -> riccastro
- Albergo -> alberg~~o~~ -> alberguccio

Unfortunately, also in this case, there isn't a way to tell which suffix has to be added to a certain noun. The only thing you can do is try to learn them.

Chapter 4

The verb

4.1 - Auxiliaries

Auxiliary verbs are verbs that are used to form compound tenses.

These verbs in Italian are essere – to be – and avere – to have.

Both essere and avere are irregular in the present tense. Let's see their conjugation.

ESSERE

Io	sono
Tu	sei
Lui/Lei	è
Noi	siamo
Voi	siete
Loro	sono

AVERE

Io	ho
Tu	hai
Lui/Lei	ha
Noi	abbiamo
Voi	avete
Loro	hanno

4.1.1 - Avere

Avere is used to form the compound tense of the majority of Italian verbs like fare, mangiare, pensare, etc.

However, avere can also be used alone.

When used alone avere can indicate:

- Possession of objects, and qualities.

    Examples:
    a. Paolo **ha** una Ferrari

    Paolo has a Ferrari

    b. **Ho** i capelli rossi

I have red hair

- The age of a person

    Ex: Monica **ha** 20 anni

    Monica is 20 years old

- A relationship

    Ex: **Ho** una sorella e un fratello

    I have a brother and a sister

- A feeling or a physical sensation

    Examples:

    a. **Abbiamo** fame

    We're hungry

    b. **Ho** paura

    I'm scared

4.1.2 - Essere

Essere is used to form the compound tense of many verbs like andare, rimanere, tornare, etc.

However, essere can also be used alone.

When used alone, essere is mostly used to link a subject either to a noun or to an adjective.

Examples:

a. Lui è Marco

He is Marco

b. Loro **sono** simpatici

They're nice

c. Noi **siamo** contenti

We're happy

4.1.2.1 – *Difference between essere and stare*

Stare is not an auxiliary verb. However, it's often confused with the verb essere, since both can mean *to be* in English.

If you're using this grammar as a self-study gudy, I strongly advise you to read this section after having read the whole grammar.

ESSERE

Essere is used to express:

1. Identity, nationality and profession

Exa: Io **sono** Carla. **Sono** italiana e **sono** un'insegnante
I'm Carla. I'm Italian and I'm a teacher

2. Origin

Ex: Lavoriamo a Perugia ma **siamo** di Milano
We work in Perugia, but we are from Milan

3. Physical appearance, and characteristics of something or someone

Examples:

a. Mirco è alto

Mirco is tall

b. Il divano è molto lungo

The sofa is very long

c. **Sei** davvero divertente

You're really funny

4. Location

Ex: Le chiavi **sono** in quel cassetto

The keys are in that drawer

5. Religious and political affiliation

Ex: Ajar è induista

Ajar is Hindu

6. Time and date

Examples:

a. **Sono** le cinque

It is 5 o'clock

b. **E'** l'8 di febbraio

It's February the 8th

7. Possession

Ex: L'auto rossa è di Lucia
The red car is Lucia's

8. A temporary condition and emotion

Examples:

a. **Sono** malato
I am sick

b. **Sono** arrabbiato
I'm angry

9. Opinions and personal observations

Ex: Quel maglione è sporco
That sweater is dirty

10. It's used as auxiliary in passive sentences

Ex: Il libro è stato letto per la prima volta nella biblioteca nazionale

The book has been read for the first time at the National library

11. It's used as auxiliary in the past tense of reflexive verbs

Ex: Mi **sono** pettinata e sono uscita
I brushed my hair and I went out

12. It's used as an auxiliary in the past tense of verbs like andare, venire, stare, tornare, etc.

Ex: Ieri Giacomo è andato al cinema
Yesterday Giacomo went to the movies

STARE

Stare is generally used to indicate:

1. Precise location

Ex: Le chiavi **stanno** nel cassetto
The keys are in the drawer

2. How you feel. It's used before the words *bene, male, meglio, peggio*.

Ex: **Sto** bene
I am well

3. Some idiomatic sentences

Ex: Quella gonna ti **sta** davvero bene
That skirt suits you very well

4. An order or an exhortation:

Examples:

a. **Stai** zitto!
Shut up!

b. **Stai** tranquillo!
Stay calm!

5. A position

Ex: **Stare** seduti a lungo non fa bene alla salute
Sitting for long periods is not good for your health

6. A synonym of "to fit"

Ex: La macchina è piena di valigie. Io non ci **sto**. Dove dovrei sedermi?
The car is full of suitcases. I can't fit in. Where shoud I sit?

7. That someone is available for something or agrees with someone

Example:

+ Organizziamo una festa a sorpresa per Paolo?

+ Shall we plan a surprise birthday party for Paolo?

– Sì, io ci **sto**

– I'm in

8. Stare per + infinitive

This combination of verbs means "to be on the point of/just about to"

Ex: **Stavo** per venire alla festa ma poi Marco mi ha chiamata e sono dovuta andare all'ospedale

I was about to come to the party, but then Marco called and I had to go to the hospital

9. Stare + gerund

This combination of verbs indicates an action the speaker is carrying out while s/he is talking.

Ex: Non posso uscire adesso. **Sto** studiando italiano

I can't go out now. I'm studying Italian

ESSERE AND STARE

Both of these Italian verbs are used to:

a. Express a location

Examples:

1. Le chiavi **sono** nel cassetto

The keys are in the drawer

2. Le chiavi **stanno** nel cassetto

The keys are in the drawer

b. Replace the Italian verbs restare and rimanere (to stay, to remain) – in certain situations

Examples:

1. Non posso venire. Oggi alle 10.00 **sono** al ristorante

I can't come. Today at 10 I'll be at the restaurant

2. Non posso venire. Oggi alle 10.00 **sto** al ristorante

I can't come. Today at 10 I'll be at the restaurant

If you need to see or print a summary table, you can find it on my website – sositalian.com – on this page: Italian grammar: difference between essere and stare.

4.2 - The present tense

USE

The present tense in Italian is generally used to:

1- Talk about something that is happening while one is speaking.

Example: **Fa** veramente caldo!
       It's really hot!

In the moment I'm speaking, I'm feeling that the weather is really hot.

2- Express something that is (always) true.

Example: Il sole **tramonta** a ovest
       The sun sets in the west

It's an undeniable truth that the sun always sets in the west.

3- Talk about future events, instead of using the future tense.

Example: Venerdì sera **vado** al cinema con Sabrina

       Friday night I'm going to the movies with Sabrina

In the sentence above, you can also use the future. However, when speaking, Italians generally prefer the present tense to talk about a future event.

4- Give orders instead of using the imperative.

Example: Tu adesso **mangi** e poi **fai** i compiti. Se ti avanza del tempo, poi, **puoi** uscire

       Now you eat and then you'll do your homework. If you have some time left, then you can go out

In the imperative, the same sentence would have been:

Mangia e fai i compiti. Poi, se ti avanza del tempo, esci.

FORMATION

In Italian there are regular and irregular verbs. Unfortunately, there is no way to tell if a verb is regular or irregular. The formation of the present tense of a verb changes accordingly if the verb is regular or irregular.

4.2.1 - *The present tense of regular verbs*

To form the present tense of regular verbs you replace the infinitive verb ending (-ARE, -ERE, -IRE) with one of the following suffixes:

-ARE

Io	-o
Tu	-i
Lui/Lei	-a
Noi	-iamo
Voi	-ate
Loro	-ano

Examples:

We work

Lavorare -> lavor~~are~~ -> lavor + iamo -> lavoriamo

You study

*Studiare -> studi~~are~~ -> studi + i -> stud~~i~~ + i -> studi

-ERE

Io	-o
Tu	-i

Lui/Lei	-e
Noi	-iamo
Voi	-ete
Loro	-ono

Examples:

S/he takes

Prendere -> prend~~ere~~ -> prend + e -> **prende**

They ask

Chiedere -> chied~~ere~~ -> chied + ono -> **chiedono**

-IRE

Io	-o
Tu	-i
Lui/Lei	-e
Noi	-iamo
Voi	-ite
Loro	-ono

Examples:

We feel/hear

Sentire -> sent~~ire~~ -> sent + iamo -> **sentiamo**

You sleep

Dormire -> dorm~~ire~~ -> dorm + i -> dormi

VERBS ENDING IN -IRE (Conjugation in -ISC)

Regular verbs ending in -ire can also have a different conjugation. Indeed, some verbs add -isc to some persons before adding the suffixes of the present tense that we've seen in the table above: -o, -i, -e, -iamo, -ite, -ono.

Have a look at the table below:

	-IRE
Io	-isco
Tu	-isci
Lui/Lei	-isce
Noi	-iamo
Voi	-ite
Loro	-iscono

Example:

I understand

Capire -> cap~~ire~~ -> cap+isc+o -> capisco

Unfortunately, there is no way to tell if a regular verb ending in -ire has the conjugation of the present tense in -isc.

Some of the most common Italian verbs with the conjugation in -isc are: capire, colpire, costruire, definire, dimagrire, ferire, finire, impedire, obbedire, preferire, proibire, pulire, restituire, riuscire, sparire, stupire, unire, etc.

CAPIRE

Io	capisco
Tu	capisci
Lui/Lei	capisce
Noi	capiamo
Voi	capite
Loro	capiscono

FINIRE

Io	finisco
Tu	finisci
Lui/Lei	finisce
Noi	finiamo
Voi	finite
Loro	finiscono

VERBS ENDING IN –GARE and -CARE

Verbs ending in -care and -gare add an **h** in the 2nd person singular and in the 1st person plural before adding the suffixes of the present tense.

Example:

You pray

Pregare -> preg~~are~~ -> preg + h + i -> preghi

PREGARE

Io	prego
Tu	preghi
Lui/Lei	prega
Noi	preghiamo
Voi	pregate
Loro	pregano

PESCARE

Io	pesco
Tu	peschi
Lui/Lei	pesca
Noi	peschiamo
Voi	pescate
Loro	pescano

VERBS ENDING IN -GIARE and -CIARE

Verbs ending in -ciare and -giare lose the final i in the 2nd person singular and in the 1st person plural before adding the suffixes of the present tense.

Example:

You start/begin

Cominciare -> cominciare -> cominci -> cominc + i -> tu cominci

COMINCIARE

Io	comincio
Tu	cominci
Lui/Lei	comincia
Noi	cominciamo
Voi	cominciate
Loro	cominciano

MANGIARE

Io	mangio
Tu	mangi
Lui/Lei	mangia
Noi	mangiamo
Voi	mangiate
Loro	mangiano

4.2.2 - *The present tense of irregular verbs*

There are no rules to form the present tense of irregular verbs. So, it has to be learned by heart.

In addition to the auxiliaries – see paragraph 4.1 – some irregular verbs in the present tense are:

POTERE

Io	posso
Tu	puoi
Lui/Lei	può
Noi	possiamo
Voi	potete
Loro	possono

FARE

Io	faccio
Tu	fai
Lui/Lei	fa
Noi	facciamo
Voi	fate
Loro	fanno

DARE

Io	do
Tu	dai
Lui/Lei	da
Noi	diamo
Voi	date
Loro	danno

ANDARE

Io	vado
Tu	vai
Lui/Lei	va
Noi	andiamo
Voi	andate
Loro	vanno

VOLERE

Io	voglio
Tu	vuoi
Lui/Lei	vuole
Noi	vogliamo
Voi	volete
Loro	vogliono

DOVERE

Io	devo
Tu	devi
Lui/Lei	deve
Noi	dobbiamo
Voi	dovete
Loro	devono

VENIRE

Io	vengo
Tu	vieni
Lui/Lei	viene
Noi	veniamo
Voi	venite
Loro	vengono

STARE

Io	sto
Tu	stai
Lui/Lei	sta
Noi	stiamo
Voi	state
Loro	stanno

RIMANERE

Io	rimango
Tu	rimani
Lui/Lei	rimane
Noi	rimaniamo
Voi	rimanete
Loro	rimangono

4.3 - Reflexive verbs

A verb is reflexive when the subject and the direct object are the same. So it is possible to say that the action that the reflexive verbs carry out is something that persons or animals are doing for themselves.

Ex: Si sta lavando
He's washing himself

Italian reflexive verbs are usually easily recognizable by the ending -si, attached to the infinitive.

Ex: lavarsi (to wash), vestirsi (to dress), pettinarsi (to comb), sdraiarsi (to lay down), ricordarsi (to remember), addormentarsi (to fall asleep), etc.

Let's see an example of a reflexive verb conjugated:

PERSONAL PRONOUN	REFLEXIVE PRONOUN	VERB
Io	mi	*vesto*
Tu	ti	*vesti*
Lui	si	*veste*
Lei	si	*veste*
Noi	ci	*vestiamo*
Voi	vi	*vestite*
Loro	si	*vestono*

As you can see from the table above, the conjugation of reflexive verbs is the same as that of all the other Italian verbs. The only difference is that they are also preceded by reflexive pronouns.

Reflexive pronouns are usually placed before a verb or attached to the infinitive.

Ex: **Mi** *ricordo* di te

I remember you

Ex: Voglio *ricordar***mi** di te

I want to remember you

4.4 - Modal verbs

Modal verbs are verbs that can indicate obligation, ability, permission, likelihood, willingness, etc.

In Italian there are three modal verbs: potere, dovere, volere.

Potere can usually mean can, could, be able, may, might
Dovere can usually mean must, to have to, should, ought to
Volere can usually mean to want, to wish, would like

Italian modal verbs can be followed by either a noun or a verb.

When they are followed by a verb, this verb must always be in the infinitive tense.

Ex: Non posso venire alla festa (I can't come to the party)
    Devo andare dal dentista domani (I've to go to the dentist tomorrow)
    Voglio comprare quel vestito (I want to buy that dress)

CONJUGATION AT THE PRESENT TENSE

POTERE

Io	posso
Tu	puoi
Lui/Lei	può
Noi	possiamo
Voi	potete
Loro	possono

DOVERE

Io	devo
Tu	devi
Lui/Lei	deve
Noi	dobbiamo
Voi	dovete
Loro	devono

VOLERE

Io	voglio
Tu	vuoi
Lui/Lei	vuole
Noi	vogliamo
Voi	volete
Loro	vogliono

4.4.1 - Potere

Potere is usually followed by a verb in the infinitive.

Potere can be generally used to:

a. Express the ability or the possibility to do something

Ex: Io **posso** aiutarti a finire l'esercizio
I can help you finish the exercise

b. Express the permission to do something

Ex: **Possiamo** andare al cinema stasera?
Can we go to the movies tonight?

c. Ask something in a gentle way

Ex: **Posso** avere un bicchiere d'acqua, per favore?
Can I have a glass of water, please?

4.4.2 - Dovere

Dovere is usually followed by a verb in the infinitive.

Dovere can be usually used to:

a. Express an obligation

Ex: **Devi** mettere la cintura quando guidi
You must wear a seatbelt when driving

b. Express the necessity to do something

Ex: **Devo** andare dal medico
I need to go to the doctor

c. Give advice and suggestions

Ex: **Devi** mangiare meno se vuoi perdere un po' di peso
You should eat less if you want to lose some weight

4.4.3 - Volere

Volere is usually followed either by a noun, a pronoun, or by a verb in the infinitive.

Volere can be usually used to:

a. Express the desire, the will to do something

Ex: **Voglio** andare in vacanza in Italia

I want to go on vacation to Italy

b. Offer something

Ex: **Vuoi** un bicchiere d'acqua?

Do you want a glass of water?

4.4.4 - Sapere

The verb sapere – to know -- can also be used as a modal verb when it expresses the ability to do something.

Ex: Maria **sa** nuotare

Maria can swim

SAPERE

Io	so
Tu	sai
Lui/Lei	sa
Noi	sappiamo
Voi	sapete
Loro	sanno

4.4.5 - Difference between sapere and potere as modal verbs

You've surely noticed that the verb potere and sapere can have a very similar meaning: they both indicate the ability to do something.

So what's the difference?

Potere is generally used when the ability to do something depends on the willingness of people or on the possibility of doing something.

Examples:

Posso aiutarti (se vuoi)
I can help you (if you want)

Visto che ha smesso di piovere, **possiamo** andare in spiaggia
Since it has stopped raining, we can go to the beach

The first example above implies that if a person is willing to accept my help, I can help him/her.

The second, instead, implies that since the rain has stopped there is the possibility for us to go to the beach.

Sapere is generally used when the ability to do something has been acquired or learned. So it's generally used when talking about skills.

Ex: **So** parlare francese
I can speak French

Now try to grasp the difference between the following sentences:

1. **Posso** nuotare (I can swim)
2. **So** nuotare (I can swim/I know how to swim)

The first sentence means that I'm able to swim, but I'm not willing to do it right now, maybe because I'm tired, or the water is too cold.

The second sentence, on the other hand, means that I've acquired the skill of swimming. So, it simply states that I can swim, without any other implication.

4.4.6 - Modal verbs and atonic pronouns

Modal verbs can also be used with atonic personal pronouns. In this case, atonic pronouns can be placed before modal verbs and they can be attached to the infinitive that follows modal verbs.

Example 1: Gli devi dire quello che hai scoperto
You have to tell him what you've found out

Example 2: Devi dirgli quello che hai scoperto
You have to tell him what you've found out

In example 1, the pronoun precedes the modal verb, while in the second example, the pronoun is attached to the infinitive that follows the modal verb. The meaning of the two sentences does not change.

4.4.7 - Modal verbs with compound tenses

When modal verbs are used with compound tenses such as passato prossimo, trapassato prossimo, etc, it is necessary to make a choice about which auxiliary should be used with them.

FIRST RULE

Usually, the auxiliary used is the same that you would use with the verb in the infinitive that follows modal verbs.

Example 1: Finalmente ho potuto parlare con lui
Finally, I could speak to him

In example 1, the modal verb potere is followed by the infinitive parlare. Now, when parlare is used with compound tenses, the auxiliary used with it is avere – ho parlato, hai parlato, ha parlato, ecc.

So, the auxiliary that should be used with the verb potere in this case is avere: ho potuto parlare.

Example 2: Finalmente **sono potuta** andare da lui
Finally, I could/I was able to go to him

In example 2, on the other hand, the infinitive that follows the modal verb potere is andare. When andare is used with compound tenses, the auxiliary used with it is essere – sono andato, sei andato, è andato, etc.

So in this case, the auxiliary that should be used with the verb potere is essere: sono potuta andare.

SECOND RULE

However, if the infinitive that follows the modal verb is intransitive – it doesn't allow an object after it – you can generally choose to use either essere or avere to form the compound tense of a modal verb.

Example 3: Ieri Giulia **è dovuta** partire per New York
Yesterday Giulia had to leave for New York

In example 3, the modal verb dovere is followed by the infinitive partire. Partire is an intransitive verb.

So, in this case, the same sentence can also be written as: Ieri Giulia ha dovuto partire per New York. The meaning of the sentence doesn't change.

ATTENTION

If modal verbs are used with both compound tenses and <u>atonic personal pronouns</u>, you should generally follow the first rule explained above.

Ex: Non <u>ci</u> **ha potuto** comprare il libro che volevamo perché era esaurito

He couldn't buy us the book we wanted because it was sold out

Ex: Non **ha potuto** comprar<u>ci</u> il libro che volevamo perché era esaurito

He couldn't buy us the book we wanted because it was sold out

4.5 - The imperative

USE

The imperative in Italian has many functions.

It is used to:

a. Give an order or a command

Ex: **Fai** quello che ti ho detto!
Do what I said!

b. Scold or reprimand:

Ex: **Vergognatevi!**
Shame on you!

c. Urge, invite, beg, or ask somebody to do something:

Examples:

Ti prego, non **spararmi**!
Please, don't shoot me!

Vieni, ti compro un gelato

Come on, I'll buy you an ice-cream

4.5.1 - Formation of regular verbs

To form the imperative of regular verbs, just replace the infinitive verb ending -are, -ere, -ire with one of the followings:

-ARE

Tu	-a
Lui/lei	-i
Noi	-iamo
Voi	-ate
Loro	-ino

Remember that in the imperative you never use personal subject pronouns in Italian.

Example:

Pensare (to think)

Pensare -> pensare -> pens + a -> pensa

-ERE

Tu	-i
Lui/lei	-a
Noi	-iamo
Voi	-ete
Loro	-ano

Example:

Credere (to believe)

Credere -> cred~~ere~~ -> cred + ano -> **credano**

-IRE

Tu	-i
Lui/Lei	-a
Noi	-iamo
Voi	-ite
Loro	-ano

Example:

Dormire (to sleep)

Dormire -> dorm~~ire~~ -> dorm + ite -> **dormite**

4.5.2 - Formation of irregular verbs

There are no formation rules to form the imperative of irregular verbs. So, the imperative of irregular verbs has to be learned by heart.

Some examples of irregular verbs in the imperative are: Essere, Avere, Dire, Fare, Stare, Sapere, Andare, Dare

ESSERE

Tu	sii
Lui/Lei	sia
Noi	siamo
Voi	siate
Loro	siano

AVERE

Tu	abbi
Lui/Lei	abbia
Noi	abbiamo
Voi	abbiate
Loro	abbiano

DIRE

Tu	di'/dì
Lui/Lei	dica

Noi	diciamo
Voi	dite
Loro	dicano

FARE

Tu	fa'/fai
Lui/Lei	faccia
Noi	facciamo
Voi	fate
Loro	facciano

STARE

Tu	sta'/stai
Lui/Lei	stia
Noi	stiamo
Voi	state
Loro	stiano

SAPERE

Tu	sappi
Lui/Lei	sappia
Noi	sappiamo
Voi	sappiate
Loro	sappiano

ANDARE

Tu	va'/vai
Lui/Lei	vada
Noi	andiamo
Voi	andate
Loro	vadano

DARE

Tu	da'/dai
Lui/Lei	dia
Noi	diamo
Voi	date
Loro	diano

4.5.3 - The imperative and tonic and atonic personal pronouns

When the 2nd person singular and the 1st and 2nd person plural of the **imperative** are followed by *tonic* or *atonic personal pronouns*, these pronouns <u>must</u> combine with the imperative.

Examples:

a. Mangia la mela -> **mangia**/*la*
Eat the apple -> Eat it

b. Mangiamo la mela -> **mangiamo**/*la*

Let's eat the apple -> Let's eat it

c. Mangiate la mela -> **mangiate**/*la*

Eat the apple -> Eat it

On the other hand, in the 3rd person singular and plural the pronouns are placed before the verb:

Examples:

a. Mangi la mela! -> *la* **mangi**!
b. Mangino la mela! -> *la* **mangino**!

4.6 - The past participle

USE

If the past participle is used alone, it always agrees with the subject.

Past participle can indicate:

a. A cause

Ex: **Accortasi** dell'errore, si scusò

Realizing her mistake, she apologized

So she apologized only because she realized her mistake.

b. A condition

Ex: **Assunto** con moderazione, il vino può dare dei benefici all'organismo
If drunk in moderation, wine may be beneficial to health

So only on condition that you drink wine in moderation, can it be beneficial to health.

c. A specific moment

Ex: Appena **rientrato**, si era accorto che qualcosa non andava
As soon as he got home, he realized that something was wrong

So, it was in the moment he got home that he realized something was wrong.

4.6.1 - Position and agreement

Past participle generally follows auxiliaries and it always agrees with the subject.

Ex: Marica è **partita**
Marica has left

In the example above, the subject, Marica, is feminine singular, so the past participle agrees with it: partita.

Exceptions:

a. When the past participle is used with the auxiliary avere or with impersonal verbs, it remains unchanged.

Examples:
Ho appena **mangiato**
I've just eaten

Oggi è **nevicato**
It snowed today

b. When the past participle is used with the pronouns *lo, la, li, le, ne*, it always agrees with them – even if the auxiliary is avere.

Ex: *Li* ha visti mentre scappavano
S/he saw them while they were running away

4.6.2 – Formation of regular verbs

To form the past participle of regular verbs, you replace the infinitive verb ending (-are, -ere, -ire) with one of the followings:

-ARE	**-ERE**	**-IRE**
-ato	-uto	-ito

Examples:
Andare -> and~~are~~ -> andato
Perdere -> perd~~ere~~ -> perduto
Dormire -> dorm~~ire~~ -> dormito

4.6.3 – Formation of irregular verbs

There are no formation rules to form the past participle of irregular verbs, so it has to be learned by heart.

Some examples of irregular verbs in the past participle are:
Essere: stato

Avere: avuto

Dare: dato

Stare: stato

Correre: corso

Fare: fatto

Ridere: riso

Rimanere: rimasto

Perdere: perso

Piacere: piaciuto

Vedere: visto

Dire: detto

Mettere: messo

Venire: venuto

4.7 - Passato prossimo

Passato prossimo in Italian can have different functions.

It can be used to:

a. Indicate events that happened in the past but still affects the present. These events can have a temporal or emotional closeness to the speaker.

Examples:

Perché non provi a sciare? Perché due anni fa **mi sono rotto** una gamba (emotional)

Why don't you try skiing? Because two years ago I broke my leg

Sono rientrato poco fa dal lavoro (temporal)

I've just returned home from work

b. Indicate a temporary action or an action that is not carried out as a habit.

Ex: Oggi **ho corso** per 10 km

I ran for 10 km today

c. Indicate a physical, emotional, or mental change.

Ex: Dopo aver dato l'esame **mi sono sentita** molto più rilassata

After having taken the exam, I felt much more relaxed

4.7.1 - Formation

Passato prossimo is formed with the present tense of either the verb *Essere* or the verb *Avere* + *Past Participle*

In most cases *to have* is the auxiliary to be used. *To be* is used with reflexive, passive, and some intransitive verbs – i.e. nascere, partire, arrivare, rientrare, entrare, etc.

Some examples:

RIMANERE

Io	sono rimasto
Tu	sei rimasto
Lui/Lei	è rimasto
Noi	siamo rimasti
Voi	siete rimasti
Loro	sono rimasti

NASCERE

Io	sono nato
Tu	sei nato
Lui/Lei	è nato
Noi	siamo nati
Voi	siete nati
Loro	sono nati

VENIRE

Io	sono venuto
Tu	sei venuto

Lui/Lei	è venuto
Noi	siamo venuti
Voi	siete venuti
Loro	sono venuti

VEDERE

Io	ho visto
Tu	hai visto
Lui/Lei	ha visto
Noi	abbiamo visto
Voi	avete visto
Loro	hanno visto

DIRE

Io	ho detto
Tu	hai detto
Lui/Lei	ha detto
Noi	abbiamo detto
Voi	avete detto
Loro	hanno detto

PRENDERE

Io	ho preso
Tu	hai preso
Lui/Lei	ha preso

Noi	abbiamo preso
Voi	avete preso
Loro	hanno preso

DARE

Io	ho dato
Tu	hai dato
Lui/Lei	ha dato
Noi	abbiamo dato
Voi	avete dato
Loro	hanno dato

POTERE

Io	ho potuto
Tu	hai potuto
Lui/Lei	ha potuto
Noi	abbiamo potuto
Voi	avete potuto
Loro	hanno potuto

SCRIVERE

Io	ho scritto
Tu	hai scritto
Lui/Lei	ha scritto
Noi	abbiamo scritto

Voi	avete scritto
Loro	hanno scritto

FARE

Io	ho fatto
Tu	hai fatto
Lui/Lei	ha fatto
Noi	abbiamo fatto
Voi	avete fatto
Loro	hanno fatto

SPENDERE

Io	ho speso
Tu	hai speso
Lui/Lei	ha speso
Noi	abbiamo speso
Voi	avete speso
Loro	hanno speso

4.7.2 - *Passato prossimo and atonic personal pronouns*

If passato prossimo is formed with the verb *to have* and is preceded by an atonic personal pronoun in the 3rd person singular or plural – lo, la, li, le – it must agree in gender and number with the pronoun.

Ex: Hai preso le **chiavi**? No, **le ha prese** Giacomo
Did you take the keys? No, Giacomo took them

In the example above the pronoun *le* is feminine plural, so the past participle must be feminine plural, too, *prese*.

If passato prossimo is formed with the verb *to have* and is preceded by an atonic personal pronoun in the 1st or 2nd person singular or plural – mi, ti, ci, vi – it can or cannot agree in gender and number with the pronoun. The choice is up to you.

Ex: Gina **ci ha visti**/Gina **ci ha visto**
Gina saw us

4.7.3 - *Passato prossimo and reflexive verbs*

Passato prossimo of reflexive verbs is always formed with the auxiliary essere. For this reason, if you form passato prossimo with a reflexive verb, the past participle has always to agree in gender and number with the subject.

Examples:

a. Francesca e Sabrina **si sono pettinate** e sono uscite
Francesca and Sabrina combed their hair and went out

b. Marco **si è pettinato** ed è uscito
Marco combed his hair and went out

In example "a" the subject is feminine plural, so the past participle must be feminine plural, too, *pettinate*.

In example "b," on the other hand, the subject is masculine singular, so the past participle must also be masculine singular, *pettinato*.

4.8 – The imperfetto

USE

Imperfetto in Italian has many different uses.

It can be used:

1. To indicate an event that happened in the past.

Ex: Mio fratello **aveva** un gatto, tanti anni fa
My brother had a cat many years ago

2. To indicate a past habit or a past action that the subject did always or frequently.

Ex: Da bambina **andavo** sempre al parco col mio papà
When I was a child, I always used to go to the park with my dad

3. To indicate an action that was being carried out when another event happened.

Ex: **Guardavo** la televisione, quando qualcuno bussò alla porta
I was watching television when someone knocked at the door

4. To tell or describe someone's dream.

Ex: Ho sognano che **ero** in mezzo all'oceano e...
I dreamed I was in the middle of the ocean and...

5. To make a request in a more gentle way.

Ex: **Volevo** tre arance e quattro mele
I wanted three oranges and four apples

6. To express in an informal way a condition or a consequence.

Ex: Se mi **telefonavi, venivo** a prenderti
If you had called me, I would have come and gotten you

7. To describe the features of people, things or places.

Ex: **Era** una donna interessante. **Aveva** lunghi capelli neri e occhi verdi, e **sorrideva** sempre
She was an interesting woman. She had long black hair and green eyes, and she always smiled

8. After using a past tense.

Ex: L'<u>ho visto</u> mentre **scappava**

4.8.1 – Formation of regular verbs

To form imperfetto of regular verbs you replace the infinitive verb ending (-ARE, -ERE, -IRE) with one of the followings:

-ARE

Io	-avo
Tu	-avi
Lui/Lei	-ava
Noi	-avamo
Voi	-avate
Loro	-avano

Example:

Pensare -> pens~~are~~ -> pens + ava -> **pensava**

-ERE

Io	-evo
Tu	-evi
Lui/Lei	-eva
Noi	-evamo
Voi	-evate
Loro	-evano

Example:

Avere -> av~~ere~~ -> av + evamo -> **avevamo**

-IRE

Io	-ivo
Tu	-ivi
Lui/Lei	-iva
Noi	-ivamo
Voi	-ivate
Loro	-ivano

Example:

Venire -> ven~~ire~~ -> ven + ivi -> **venivi**

4.8.2 – Formation of irregular verbs

To form imperfetto of irregular verbs there are no formation rules. So, it has to be learned by heart.

Some examples of irregular verbs in the imperfetto tense are:

ESSERE

Io	ero
Tu	eri

Lui/Lei	era
Noi	eravamo
Voi	eravate
Loro	erano

DIRE

Io	dicevo
Tu	dicevi
Lui/Lei	diceva
Noi	dicevamo
Voi	dicevate
Loro	dicevano

FARE

Io	facevo
Tu	facevi
Lui/Lei	faceva
Noi	facevamo
Voi	facevate
Loro	facevano

DARE

Io	davo
Tu	davi
Lui/Lei	dava

Noi	davamo
Voi	davate
Loro	davano

4.9 - Difference between imperfetto and passato prossimo

Sometimes it can be difficult to understand the difference between imperfetto and passato prossimo because these two tenses are used in a very similar way.

Let's see the main differences between imperfetto and passato prossimo.

1) PAST HABITS VS RARE PAST ACTIONS

Imperfetto is used to indicate a past habit or an action that the subject did frequently in the past.

Examples:

a. La domenica **andavo** sempre in chiesa
On Sundays I always went to church

b. Mia madre **cucinava** spesso le lasagne
My mother used to cook lasagna often

In example "a" I'm saying that in the past it was a habit for me to go to church on Sundays.

In example "b," on the other hand, I'm saying that it was frequent for my mother to cook lasagna in the past.

Passato prossimo, on the other hand, is used to indicate a past action which wasn't carried out frequently or more than once in the past and that still affects the present.

Examples:

a. Ieri **sono andato** in chiesa
Yesterday I went to church

b. Mia madre **ha appena** cucinato le lasagne
My mother has just cooked lasagna

In example "a" I'm stressing the fact that I went to church only yesterday. It's certainly not a habit for me to go to church.

In example "b," on the other hand, I'm saying that my mother has just cooked lasagna. I can be expressing both the fact that my mother usually doesn't cook lasagna, and the fact that the smell of lasagna is still fresh in the air.

2) DESCRIPTION OF PAST CONDITIONS VS CHANGE OF CONDITION IN THE PAST

Imperfetto is used to describe emotional, physical, or meteorological conditions.

Examples:

a. Ieri **ero** stanchissimo
 I was really tired yesterday (physical condition)

b. Ieri **ero** triste
I was sad yesterday (emotional condition)

c. Ieri **pioveva**
It rained yesterday (meteorological condition)

Passato prossimo, on the other hand, is used to indicate a physical, emotional, or mental change that happened in the past.

Ex: Dopo aver dato l'esame **mi sono sentita** molto più rilassata
After having taken the exam, I felt much more relaxed

Before the exam I was worried and stressed. After taking it, I felt much more relaxed. So there was a physical, emotional, and mental change.

Finally, passato prossimo is also generally used in descriptions after words such as *così, allora, dunque,* e *quindi.*

Ex: **Pioveva**, così siamo rimasti a casa
It was raining, so we stayed home

4.10 - How to talk about actions that happened at the same time

When two events happened at the same time in the past, you can use:

1. **imperfetto + imperfetto** -> indicates two events that lasted for a medium or long time. It's not clear if the second event – mio marito faceva ginnastica – ended before the end of the first event or it kept going on.

Ex: Mentre **leggevo** un libro, mio marito **faceva** ginnastica
While I was reading a book, my husband was working out

Did my husband stop working out when I stopped reading or did he keep working out?

2. **imperfetto + passato prossimo** -> indicates two events. One that lasted for a medium or long time – the one expressed by the imperfetto – and the other one that lasted for a short time – the one expressed by

passato prossimo. The event expressed by passato prossimo ended before the end of the event expressed by imperfetto or at the same time.

Ex: Mentre leggevo un libro, mio marito ha fatto ginnastica

While I was reading a book, my husband worked out

3. **imperfetto + passato prossimo** -> indicates an event that lasted for a medium or long time, but was interrupted by another event that lasted for a short time.

Mentre passeggiavo, ho visto Marta

While I was taking a stroll, I saw Marta

Mentre leggevo, è squillato il telefono

While I was reading, the phone rang

4.11 – Phraseological verbs

Phraseological verbs are verbs that if used with infinitives or gerund can indicate:

1. AN ONGOING ACTION

a. Stare + gerundio. *Stare* is usually used in the presente and in the imperfetto tense.

Ex: Non disturbarla, **sta/stava facendo** i compiti
Don't bother her, she is/was doing her homework

2. A FORTHCOMING ACTION

a. **Stare per + infinito**

Ex: Maria **stava per andarsene**, poi ha cambiato idea
Maria was about to leave, then she changed her mind

b. **Essere lì lì per + infinito**

Ex: Maria **era lì lì per andarsene**, poi ha cambiato idea
Maria was about to leave, then she changed her mind

c. **Essere sul punto di + infinito**

Ex: Maria **era sul punto di andarsene**, poi ha cambiato idea
Maria was about to leave, then she changed her mind

d. **Essere in procinto di + infinito** (formale)

Ex: Maria **era in procinto di andarsene**, poi ha cambiato idea
Maria was about to leave, then she changed her mind

e. **Accingersi a + infinito** (formale)

Ex: Maria **si accinse ad andarsene**, ma poi cambiò idea

Maria was about to leave, then she changed her mind

3. THE START OF AN ACTION

a. **Cominciare a + infinito**

Ex: Era tranquillo, poi **ha cominciato a piangere**

He was quiet, then he started to cry

b. **Iniziare a + infinito**

Ex: Era tranquillo, poi **ha iniziato a piangere**

He was quiet, then he started to cry

c. **Mettersi a + infinito**

Ex: Era tranquillo, poi **si è messo a piangere**

He was quiet, then he started to cry

4. THE CONTINUATION OF AN ACTION

a. **Continuare a + infinito**

Ex: Luca **continuò a leggere**

Luca kept reading

b. **Andare avanti a + infinito**

Ex: Luca **andò avanti a leggere**
Luca kept reading

5. THE END OF AN ACTION
a. **Finire di + infinito**

Ex: Avete **finito di fare** l'esercizio?
Have you finished the exercise?

b. **Smettere di + infinito**

Ex: Abbiamo **smesso di fumare**
We stopped smoking

c. **Finirla di + infinito** (informale)

Ex: **Finitela di urlare!**
Stop screaming!

d. **Piantarla di + infinito** (informale)

Ex: **Piantatela di urlare!**

Stop screaming!

4.12 - The simple future

USE

The future tense is used to:

1- Talk about facts that will happen in the future.

Ex: Domani **andrò** al cinema
Tomorrow I'm going to the movies

However, Italians don't use this tense very much, preferring instead the present tense. When the present tense is used to talk about future events, it is generally preceded or followed by a time expression – domani, l'anno prossimo, tra un mese, etc.

Examples:

a. Fra poco arrivo
I'll be there soon

b. L'anno prossimo andiamo a Parigi
Next year we're going to Paris

2- Talk about a probability or a guess

Examples:

a. Le luci sono spente, **sarà** uscito
The lights are off; he must be out

b. Sua sorella **avrà** 16 anni
His sister is probably 16 years old

3- Express a command

Ex: La prossima volta che **avrete** un problema, vi <u>rivolgerete</u> a me
Next time you have a problem, you'll speak to me

4- Apologize

Ex: Lei mi **scuserà** ma devo proprio andare
I'm sorry, but I really have to leave

5- Make a concession. Concessive clauses are those clauses that can signal a contrast, a qualification, or a concession in relation to the idea expressed in the main clause

Examples:

a. Giulia **sarà** anche intelligente, ma a me sta antipatica

Giulia may be intelligent, but I find her unpleasant

b. Il caffè **farà** anche bene, ma a me non piace
Coffee may be healthy, but I don't like it

4.12.1 – Formation of regular verbs

To form the simple future of regular verbs, replace the infinitive verb ending (-ARE, -ERE, -IRE) with one of the followings:

-ARE

Io	-erò
Tu	-erai
Lui/Lei	-erà
Noi	-eremo
Voi	-erete
Loro	-eranno

Example:
Pensare -> pens~~are~~ -> pens + erà -> lui **penserà**

-ERE

Io	-erò
Tu	-erai
Lui/Lei	-erà

Noi	-eremo
Voi	-erete
Loro	-eranno

Example:

Credere -> cred~~ere~~ -> cred + eremo -> noi **crederemo**

-IRE

Io	-irò
Tu	-irai
Lui/Lei	-irà
Noi	-iremo
Voi	-irete
Loro	-iranno

Example:

Finire -> fin~~ire~~ -> fin + iranno -> loro **finiranno**

4.12.2 – Formation of irregular verbs

There are no formation rules to form the simple future of irregular verbs. So it has to be learned by heart.

Some examples of irregular verbs in the simple future tense are:

ESSERE

Io	sarò
Tu	sarai
Lui/Lei	sarà
Noi	saremo
Voi	sarete
Loro	saranno

AVERE

Io	avrò
Tu	avrai
Lui/Lei	avrà
Noi	avremo
Voi	avrete
Loro	avranno

ANDARE

Io	andrò
Tu	andrai
Lui/Lei	andrà
Noi	andremo
Voi	andrete
Loro	andranno

POTERE

Io	potrò
Tu	potrai
Lui/Lei	potrà
Noi	potremo
Voi	potrete
Loro	potranno

SAPERE

Io	saprò
Tu	saprai
Lui/Lei	saprà
Noi	sapremo
Voi	saprete
Loro	sapranno

VEDERE

Io	vedrò
Tu	vedrai
Lui/Lei	vedrà
Noi	vedremo
Voi	vedrete
Loro	vedranno

VIVERE

Io	vivrò
Tu	vivrai
Lui/Lei	vivrà
Noi	vivremo
Voi	vivrete
Loro	vivranno

DOVERE

Io	dovrò
Tu	dovrai
Lui/Lei	dovrà
Noi	dovremo
Voi	dovrete
Loro	dovranno

VENIRE

Io	verrò
Tu	verrai
Lui/Lei	verrà
Noi	verremo
Voi	verrete
Loro	verranno

VOLERE

Io	vorrò
Tu	vorrai
Lui/Lei	vorrà
Noi	vorremo
Voi	vorrete
Loro	vorranno

DARE

Io	darò
Tu	darai
Lui/Lei	darà
Noi	daremo
Voi	darete
Loro	daranno

STARE

Io	starò
Tu	starai
Lui/Lei	starà
Noi	staremo
Voi	starete
Loro	staranno

FARE

Io	farò
Tu	farai
Lui/Lei	farà
Noi	faremo
Voi	farete
Loro	faranno

4.12.3 - *Verbs ending in -care, -gare*

Verbs ending in -care and -gare form the simple future by removing the suffix -are and adding an "h" before adding the suffix of the future. In this way, the hard sound of letters "g" and "c" is retained.

Examples:

Cercare -> cerc~~are~~ -> cerc + h -> io cercherò

Pregare -> preg~~are~~ -> preg + h -> noi pregheremo

CERCARE

Io	cercherò
Tu	cercherai
Lui/Lei	cercherà
Noi	cercheremo
Voi	cercherete
Loro	cercheranno

PREGARE

Io	pregherò
Tu	pregherai
Lui/Lei	pregherà
Noi	pregheremo
Voi	pregherete
Loro	pregheranno

4.12.4 - Verbs ending in -ciare, -giare

Verbs ending in -ciare and -giare form the simple future by removing the suffix -are and dropping the -i before adding the suffix of the future.

Examples:

Cominciare -> cominci~~are~~ -> cominc~~i~~ -> tu comincerai

Mangiare -> mangi~~are~~ -> mang~~i~~ -> loro mangeranno

COMINCIARE

Io	comincerò
Tu	comincerai
Lui/Lei	comincerà
Noi	cominceremo
Voi	comincerete
Loro	cominceranno

MANGIARE

Io	mangerò
Tu	mangerai
Lui/Lei	mangerà
Noi	mangeremo
Voi	mangerete
Loro	mangeranno

4.13 - The present conditional

USE

Independent clauses are clauses that can stand by themselves. They don't contain words such as senza che, perché, etc. The present conditional is used to:

- Ask something in a gentle way

    Ex: **Vorrei** una pizza margherita
    I'd like a pizza margherita

- Say something in a gentle way, whether it's an order, an opinion, or a piece of advice

    Ex: **Dovresti** mangiare meno
    You should eat less

Ex: **Sarebbe** meglio lasciar perdere
We'd better give up

- Present an event as possible or probable (in newspapers or on TV)

Ex: Berlusconi **dovrebbe** partire per New York la prossima settimana.
Berlusconi should leave for New York next week

- Make a wish

Ex: Mi **piacerebbe** andare in vacanza alle Maldive l'anno prossimo.
I'd like to go on vacation to Maldives next year

USE IN DEPENDENT CLAUSES

In dependent clauses – clauses that cannot stand on their own – the conditional is usually used to:

- Ask an indirect question

Ex: Mi domando se ti **andrebbe** una fetta di torta

I'm wondering if you'd like a piece of cake

- Express a cause

    Ex: Ti chiamo perché mi **piacerebbe** uscire a cena con te
    I'm calling you because I'd like to go out to dinner with you

- Express a contrast

    Ex: Stai ancora dormendo mentre **saresti** già dovuto essere al lavoro
    You're still sleeping when you should be working now

4.13.1 – Formation of regular verbs

To form the present conditional of regular verbs, you replace the suffixes **-are**, **-ere**, **-ire** with one of the following suffixes:

-ARE

Io	-erei
Tu	-eresti
Lui/Lei	-erebbe
Noi	-eremmo
Voi	-ereste
Loro	-erebbero

Example:

He would talk

Parlare -> parl~~are~~ -> parl + erebbe -> **parlerebbe**

-ERE

Io	-erei
Tu	-eresti
Lui/Lei	-erebbe
Noi	-eremmo
Voi	-ereste
Loro	-erebbero

Example:

They would believe

Credere -> cred~~ere~~ -> cred + erebbero -> **crederebbero**

-IRE

Io	-irei
Tu	-iresti
Lui/Lei	-irebbe
Noi	-iremmo
Voi	-ireste

Loro	-irebbero

Example:

I would finish

Finire -> fin~~ire~~ -> fin + irei -> finirei

4.13.2 – Formation of irregular verbs

There are no formation rules to form the present conditional of irregular verbs. They have to be learned by heart.

Some examples of irregular verbs in the present conditional are:

ESSERE

Io	sarei
Tu	saresti
Lui/Lei	sarebbe
Noi	saremmo
Voi	sareste
Loro	sarebbero

AVERE

Io	avrei
Tu	avresti

Lui/Lei	avrebbe
Noi	avremmo
Voi	avreste
Loro	avrebbero

POTERE

Io	potrei
Tu	potresti
Lui/Lei	potrebbe
Noi	potremmo
Voi	potreste
Loro	potrebbero

SAPERE

Io	saprei
Tu	sapresti
Lui/Lei	saprebbe
Noi	sapremmo
Voi	sapreste
Loro	saprebbero

VENIRE

Io	verrei
Tu	verresti
Lui/Lei	verrebbe

Noi	verremmo
Voi	verreste
Loro	verrebbero

VOLERE

Io	vorrei
Tu	vorresti
Lui/Lei	vorrebbe
Noi	vorremmo
Voi	vorreste
Loro	vorrebbero

STARE

Io	starei
Tu	staresti
Lui/Lei	starebbe
Noi	staremmo
Voi	stareste
Loro	starebbero

FARE

Io	farei
Tu	faresti
Lui/Lei	farebbe
Noi	faremmo

Voi fareste
Loro farebbero

4.13.3 - Verbs ending in -care, -gare

Verbs ending in -care and -gare form the present conditional by removing the suffix -are and adding an "h" before adding the suffix of the conditional. In this way, the hard sound of letters "g" and "c" is retained.

Examples:
Cercare -> cerc~~are~~ -> cerc + h -> io **cercherei**
Pregare -> preg~~are~~ -> preg + h -> noi **pregheremmo**

CERCARE

Io	cercherei
Tu	cercheresti
Lui/Lei	cercherebbe
Noi	cercheremmo
Voi	cerchereste
Loro	cercherebbero

PREGARE

Io	pregherei
Tu	pregheresti

Lui/Lei	pregherebbe
Noi	pregheremmo
Voi	preghereste
Loro	pregherebbero

4.13.4 - *Verbs ending in -ciare, -giare*

Verbs ending in -ciare and -giare form the present conditional by removing the suffix -are and dropping the -i before adding the suffix of the conditional.

Examples:

Cominciare -> cominci~~are~~ -> cominc~~i~~ -> tu cominceresti

Mangiare -> mangi~~are~~ -> mang~~i~~ -> loro mangerebbero

COMINCIARE

Io	comincerei
Tu	cominceresti
Lui/Lei	comincerebbe
Noi	cominceremmo
Voi	comincereste
Loro	comincerebbero

MANGIARE

Io	mangerei
Tu	mangeresti
Lui/Lei	mangerebbe
Noi	mangeremmo
Voi	mangereste
Loro	mangerebbero

Chapter 5
The articles

5.1 - Definite articles

In English there's only one definite article: the. In Italian, on the other hand, there are several definite articles. Their usage depends on the gender and number of the word preceding them.

	SINGULAR	PLURAL
FEMININE	La	Le
	L'	Le
MASCULINE	Il	I
	Lo	Gli
	L'	Gli

5.1.1 - Feminine singular

For feminine singular nouns you must choose between la and l'.

La is used with words starting with **consonant**

L' is used with words starting with **vowel or h**

    La casa -> the home/house
    L'acqua -> the water
    La mano -> the hand
    L'oca -> the goose

5.1.2 - Masculine singular

For masculine singular nouns you must choose between l', lo, and il.

L' is used with words starting with **vowel or h**

Lo is used with words starting with **z**, **gn**, **ps**, **pn**, **x**, **s + consonant**, and **y/j/i + vowel**

Il is used with **all the other masculine words**

    L'uomo -> the man

Lo **sc**opo -> the aim

Lo **gn**occo -> the gnocco

Il lago -> the lake

5.1.3 - Feminine plural

Le is used with **every plural feminine word**.

Le **case** -> the houses/homes

Le **acque** -> the waters

Le **mani** -> the hands

Le **oche** -> the geese

5.1.4 - Masculine plural

Gli is the plural of **lo** and **l'**.

So, gli is used with plural words starting with **vowel**, and with **z, gn, ps, x, y, s + consonant, i + vowel**.

I, finally, is the plural of **il**. So, it is used with **all the other masculine plural words**.

Gli **u**omini -> the men

Gli **sc**opi -> the aims

Gli **gn**occhi -> the gnocchi

I laghi -> the lakes

5.1.5 - Use

The use of definite articles in Italian is often very similar to that of their equivalent in English.

However, there are also some differences:

1. Italian uses definite articles before a noun used in a general sense:

Ex: I pinguini vivono al polo sud
Penguins live in the South Pole

2. Italian uses definite articles before a title followed by a surname:

Ex: La signora Rossi è la mia vicina
Ms Rossi is my neighbour

However, if you address a person directly, you do not use the article:

Examples:

a. Buongiorno, dottore
Good morning, doctor

b. Buongiorno, signora Rossi

Good morning, Ms Rossi

3. Italian uses definite articles before years:

Ex: Il 2015, il 1980, il 1435…

4. Italian, sometimes, uses definite articles where English uses possessives articles, indefinite articles, or where English doesn't use an article at all:

Ex:

a. Mi fa male la gamba

I hurt my leg

b. Marica ha il naso lungo

Marica has a long nose

c. Marica ha i capelli biondi

Marica has blond hair

5. Finally, Italian uses definite articles before countries and regions. However, if a preposition is used, the article is not always used:

Ex:

a. L'italia è un bel paese

Italy is a beautiful country

b. **In** Italia c'è il colosseo
In Italy there is the Colosseum

5.2 - Indefinite articles

Italian indefinite articles correspond to the English a, an.

In Italian indefinite articles are used to:

1. Talk about someone or something in a generic way.

Ex: Prendi **una** sedia e siediti
Take a chair and sit

2. Refer to something for the first time.

Ex: Ho conosciuto **un** ragazzo davvero simpatico
I've met a really nice guy

3. Refer to a specific member of a group or class.

Ex: Marco è **un** chirurgo
Marco is a surgeon

Indefinite articles have only a singular form. In Italian the use of indefinite articles depends on the gender of the word following them.

5.2.1 - Feminine indefinite articles

Una	Un'
Ex: **Una** casa	Ex: **Un'a**natra
A house	A duck

As it's possible to notice from the table above, we use **un'** with feminine singular nouns starting with a vowel. We use **una** for all the others feminine singular nouns.

5.2.2 - Masculine indefinite articles

Un	Uno
Ex: **Un** sogno	Ex: **Uno** gnomo
A dream	A duck
Ex: **Un o**cchio	Ex: **Uno ps**icologo
An eye	A psychologist

We use **uno** with masculine singular nouns starting with **z**, **gn**, **ps**, **pn**, **x**, **s + consonant**, and **y/j/i + vowel**. We use **un** for all the others masculine singular nouns.

5.3 - Partitive articles

Partitive articles are articles used to indicate an unspecified amount or quantity.

Ex: Sto mangiando **della** frutta
I'm eating some fruit

In Italian there are six partitive articles: del, dello, della, dei, degli, delle.

	PARTITIVE ARTICLES
MASCULINE SINGULAR	dell', dello, del
FEMININE SINGULAR	della, dell'
MASCULINE PLURAL	degli, dei
FEMININE PLURAL	delle

5.3.1 - Singular partitive articles

Singular partitive articles are used to indicate an unspecified amount or quantity related to uncountable nouns – acqua, olio, vino, musica, consigli, etc.

Singular partitive articles are formed combining the preposition **di** + <u>a definite article</u>. So, singular partitive articles change according to the gender of the noun following them.

In Italian, singular partitive articles are often replaced by the expression: *un po' di*.

Ex: Ho bevuto **del** vino ieri -> Yesterday I drank some wine
    Ho bevuto *un po' di* vino ieri -> Yesterday I drank some wine

5.3.1.1 - Masculine partitive articles

For masculine singular nouns there are three partitive articles: **dell'**, **dello** and **del**.

Dell' is used with masculine singular nouns starting with a vowel.

Ex: Attento! C'è dell'olio sul pavimento
Beware! There's some oil on the floor

Dello is used when the word that follows it starts with s + consonant, gn, x, pn, ps, and y/j/i + vowel.

Ex: Passami **dello** spago, per favore
Hand me some twine, please

Del, instead, is used in all the other case.

Ex: Vorrei **del** vino
I'd like some wine

5.3.1.2 - *Feminine partitive articles*

For feminine singular nouns there are two partitive articles: **dell'** and **della**.

Dell' is used for singular feminine nouns starting with a vowel.

Ex: Potrei avere **dell'**acqua, per favore?
Can I have some water, please?

Della, instead, is used for all the other feminine singular nouns.

Ex: Se vuoi, c'è ancora **della** marmellata in frigo
If you want, there's still some jam left in the fridge

5.3.2 - Plural partitive articles

Plural partitive articles are used to indicate an unspecified amount or quantity related to countable nouns. So, they are used to create the plural of indefinite articles – un, uno, una.

Plural partitive articles are formed combining the preposition **di** + a definite article. So, plural partitive articles change according to the gender of the noun following them.

5.3.2.1 - Masculine partitive articles

In Italian there are two possible masculine plural partitive articles: **degli** and **dei**.

Degli is considered the plural of the indefinite article uno, while **dei** is considered the plural of the indefinite article un.

Degli is used with masculine words starting with z, gn, ps, pn, x, s + consonant, and y/j/i + vowel.

Ex: Ho comprato **degli** stivali comodissimi
I bought some very comfortable boots

Dei is used in all the other cases.

Ex: Sto comprando **dei** libri

I'm buying some books

Attention Even if **dei** is considered the plural of the indefinite article un, it is not used with masculine words starting with vowels. You have to use **degli** instead.

Ex: Esco con **degli** amici

I'm going out with some friends

5.3.2.2 - Feminine partitive articles

There is only one feminine plural partitive article: **delle**.

Delle is considered the plural of the indefinite article una. **Delle** is used with every plural feminine word.

Oggi ho visto **delle** anatre al parco

Today I saw some ducks in the park

INDEFINITE ARTICLES	PARTITIVE ARTICLES
Un	**Dei**

Uno Degli
Una – Un' Delle

5.3.3 - *When partitive articles are not used*

There are some cases in which partitive articles are not generally used in Italian. In particular, they're not used:

1. In negative sentences

Examples:

a. Non ho bevuto vino ieri
I didn't drink wine yesterday

b. Non c'è più marmellata in frigo
There's no jam in the fridge anymore

2. After the prepositions da and di.

Examples:

a. Sono andante da alcune amiche
They went to meet some friends

b. Ho bisogno di alcune mele
I need some apples

Chapter 6

Numbers

6.1 - Cardinal numbers

Cardinal numbers are the most used numbers. They indicate the amount of something such as one, two, three, etc.

In Italian, numbers from 0 to 19 and the tens have to be learned by heart

6.1.1 - Numbers from 0 to 10

NUMBERS	NUMBERS IN LETTERS
0	Zero
1	Uno
2	Due
3	Tre
4	Quattro
5	Cinque
6	Sei
7	Sette
8	Otto

9	Nove
10	Dieci

6.1.2 - *Numbers from 11 to 19*

NUMBERS	NUMBERS IN LETTERS
11	Undici
12	Dodici
13	Tredici
14	Quattordici
15	Quindici
16	Sedici
17	Diciassette
18	Diciotto
19	Diciannove

6.1.3 - Tens

NUMBERS	NUMBERS IN LETTERS
20	Venti
30	Trenta
40	Quaranta
50	Cinquanta
60	Sessanta
70	Settanta
80	Ottanta
90	Novanta

6.1.4 - How to form and read numbers

Forming numbers in Italian is pretty simple.

TENS +1 OR 8

If you want to form tens plus number 1 or number 8, let's say 28 or 31, you just say the tens, you delete the last vowel of the tens and then you add the unit.

Examples:

a. 28 -> venti -> vent + otto -> Ventotto

b. 31 -> trenta -> trent + uno -> Trentuno

Just remember that this rule applies only if you want to form numbers composed of tens plus number 1 or plus number 8.

TENS + 2, 3, 4, 5, 6, 7, 9

If you want to form tens plus number 2, 3, 4, 5, 6, 7, 9, let's say 56 or 89, you just say the tens and then you add the unit.

Examples:

a. 56 -> Cinquanta + sei -> **Cinquantasei**
b. 89 -> Ottanta + nove -> **Ottantanove**

Just pay attention to all the tens plus number 3 because number three takes an acute accent on its final e.

Examples:

a. 33 -> trenta + tre -> **trentatré**
b. 73 -> settanta + tre -> **settantatré**
c. 43 -> quaranta + tre -> **quarantatré**

6.1.5 - Hundreds

NUMBERS	NUMBERS IN LETTERS
100	Cento
200	Duecento
300	Trecento
400	Quattrocento
500	Cinquecento
600	Seicento
700	Settecento
800	Ottocento
900	Novecento

If you want to form hundreds, let's say, 103, 168, 138, you say the hundreds and then you add the tens or the units.

Examples:

a. 103 -> Cento + tre -> Centotrè

b. 167 -> Cento + sessantasette -> Centosessantasette

c. 138 -> Cento + trentotto -> Centotrentotto

6.1.6 - Thousands

NUMBERS	NUMBERS IN LETTERS
1000	Mille
2000	Duemila
3000	Tremila
4000	Quattromila
5000	Cinquemila
6000	Seimila
7000	Settemila
8000	Ottomila
9000	Novemila
10000	Diecimila
11000	Undicimila

Finally, if you want to form thousands, let's say, 9845, 1241, 16.749, 4005, you say the thousands and then add the hundreds, the tens and the units.

Examples:

a. 9845 -> novemila + ottocento + quaranta + cinque -> **novemilaottocentoquarantacinque**

b. 1241 -> mille + duecento + quaranta + uno -> **milleduecentoquarantuno**

c. 16.749 -> sedicimila + settecento + quaranta + nove -> **sedicimilasettecentoquarantanove**

d. 4005 -> quattromila + cinque -> **quattromilacinque**

6.1.7 - How to read years

Years in Italian are read exactly as cardinal numbers. So, if you want to read a year, let's say 2017, you just pronounce it as duemiladiciassette.

Examples:

a. 1987 -> **Millenovecentoottantasette**
b. 1240 -> **Milleduecentoquaranta**

6.1.8 - Agreement of cardinal numbers

Cardinal numbers are invariable except number 1, which agrees in gender with the noun it refers to.

Examples:

a. Quante mele ci sono nel frigorifero? Una
How many apples are there in the fridge? One
b. Quanti meloni ci sono nel frigorifero? Uno

How many melons are there in the fridge? One

c. Quante mele ci sono nel frigorifero? Cinque

How many apples are there in the fridge? Five

In the first example the cardinal number to be used is *una* since it agrees with the noun *mela* which is feminine.

In the second example, the cardinal number to be used is *uno* since it agrees with the noun *melone* which is masculine.

Finally, in the third example, the cardinal number *cinque* doesn't change since it's invariable.

6.2 - Ordinal numbers

Ordinal numbers are numbers that tell the position of something in a list, such as first, second, third, etc.

Ordinal numbers from 1 to 10 have to be learned by heart.

NUMBERS	NUMBERS IN LETTERS
1	**Primo**
2	**Secondo**
3	**Terzo**
4	**Quarto**

5	**Quinto**
6	**Sesto**
7	**Settimo**
8	**Ottavo**
9	**Nono**
10	**Decimo**

6.2.1 - How to form and read ordinal numbers

To form any ordinal number you just say the number, delete its final letter, and add the suffix *–esimo*.

Examples:

a. 20 -> Venti -> Vent~~i~~ + esimo -> **Ventesimo**

b. 100 –> Cento -> Cent~~o~~ + esimo -> **Centesimo**

c. 5478 -> Cinquemilaquattrocentosettantotto -> Cinquemilaquattrocentosettantott~~o~~ + esimo -> **Cinquemilaquattrocentosettantottesimo**

The only exceptions are numbers that end with 3 – tre –, such as 543. In this case the final letter of the number is preserved, and you just add the suffix –esimo.

Examples:

a. 543 -> Cinquecentoquarantatre + esimo -> **Cinquecentoquarantatreesimo**
b. 1793 -> Millesettecentonovantatre + esimo -> **Millesettecentonovantatreesimo**

6.2.2 - How to read centuries

Centuries in Italian are read exactly as ordinal numbers. So, if you want to read a century, let's say XIX, you just pronounce it as diciannovesimo secolo.

Examples:

XX -> **Ventesimo secolo**
XIV -> **Quattordicesimo secolo**
VI -> **Sesto secolo**

6.2.3 - Agreement of ordinal numbers

Ordinal numbers agree in gender and number with the noun they refer to.

Examples:

a. <u>Mario</u> è arrivato <u>primo</u>

Mario finished 1st

b. <u>Lucia</u> è arrivata <u>terza</u>

Lucia finished 3rd

c. <u>Renato e Marco</u> sono arrivati <u>ventinovesimi</u>

Renato and Marco finished 29th

d. <u>Maria e Giulia</u> sono arrivate <u>centesime</u>

Maria and Giulia finished 100th

In the first example the ordinal number *primo* agrees with the noun *Mario* which is masculine singular.

In the second example, instead, the ordinal number *terza* agrees with the noun *Lucia* which is feminine singular.

In the third example, the ordinal number *ventinovesimi* agrees with the nouns *Renato* and *Marco* which are masculine plural.

Finally, in the fourth example, the ordinal number *centesime* agrees with the nouns *Maria* and *Giulia* which are feminine plural.

Chapter 7

Adjectives

Adjectives are words that define and clarify nouns.

Ex: Francesco è **bello**
Francesco is beautiful

7.1 - Feminine and masculine of adjectives

Adjectives in Italian must agree in gender and number with the noun they refer to.

If the noun is masculine singular, the adjective must be masculine singular. If the noun is feminine plural, the adjective must be feminine plural, etc.

7.1.1 - Adjectives ending in -o

Adjectives ending in **-o** in the masculine singular form the feminine singular replacing -o with -a:

MASCULINE SINGULAR	FEMININE SINGULAR
-o	-a
Ex: Ragazzo italian<u>o</u>	Ex: Ragazza italian<u>a</u>
Italian boy	Italian girl

7.1.2 - Adjectives ending in -e

Adjectives ending in -e in the masculine singular do not change in the feminine singular:

MASCULINE SINGULAR	FEMININE SINGULAR
-e	-e
Ex: Ragazzo frances<u>e</u>	Ex: Ragazza frances<u>e</u>
French boy	French girl

7.1.3 - Adjectives ending in -a

Adjectives ending in -a in the masculine singular do not change in the feminine singular:

MASCULINE SINGULAR	FEMININE SINGULAR
-a	-a
Ex: Marco è egoist<u>a</u>	Ex: Lucia è egoist<u>a</u>
Marco is selfish	Lucia is selfish

7.2 - Plural of adjectives

Let's see now how to form the plural of all the adjectives in Italian.

7.2.1 - Adjectives ending in -o

Adjectives ending in -o in the masculine singular form the masculine plural replacing -o with -i, and form the feminine plural replacing -o with -e:

Examples:

Masculine singular: Ragazzo italiano (Italian boy)
Masculine plural: Ragazzi italiani (Italian boys)
Feminine plural: Ragazze italiane (Italian girls)

However, if the adjective ends in -*co* and has a tonic accent on its second last syllable, it adds an h after "c" when it changes into the plural.

Examples:

Antico -> antichi, antiche
Cieco -> ciechi, cieche

Instead, if the adjective ends in -*co* and has a tonic accent on its third last syllable, it adds an **h** after "c" only when it changes into the feminine plural.

Examples:

Simpatico -> simpatic**h**e, simpatici
Magico -> magic**h**e, magici

Moreover, if the adjective ends in -*go*, it adds an **h** after "g" when it changes into the plural.

Examples:
Lungo -> lung**h**i, lung**h**e
Largo -> larg**h**i, larg**h**e

7.2.1.1 - Adjectives ending in -cio and -gio

Adjectives ending in **-cio** and **-gio** in the masculine singular form the masculine plural by deleting the final -o, and form the feminine plural by replacing -o with -e:

Examples:

Masculine singular: Maglione grigio (Grey sweater)
Masculine plural: Maglioni grigi (Grey sweaters)
Feminine plural: Scarpe grigie (Grey shoes)

However, if *c* and *g* are preceded by a consonant, these adjectives form the masculine plural by deleting the final -o, and the feminine plural by deleting the final -io and by adding -e.

Examples:

Masculine singular: Ragazzo saggio (Wise boy)
Masculine plural: Ragazzi saggi (Wise boys)
Feminine plural: Ragazze sagge (Wise girls)

7.2.2 - Adjectives ending in -e

Adjectives ending in -e in the masculine singular form both the masculine and the feminine plural replacing -e with -i:

Examples:

Masculine singular: Ragazzo francese (French boy)
Masculine plural: Ragazzi francesi (French boys)
Feminine plural: Ragazze francesi (French girls)

7.2.3 - Adjectives ending in -a

Adjectives ending in -a in the masculine singular form the masculine plural replacing -a with -i, and form the feminine plural replacing -a with -e:

Examples:

Masculine singular: Marco è vietnamita (Marco is Vietnamese)
Masculine plural: Marco e Fabio sono vietnamiti (Marco and Fabio are Vietnamese)
Feminine plural: Lucia e Sara sono vietnamite (Lucia and Sara are Vietnamese)

This group of adjectives includes, especially, adjectives ending in *–ista, -cida, -ita*.

7.2.4 - Other information

If the adjective refers to both a masculine and a feminine noun, it usually takes a masculine form.

Ex: Ho comprato due maglie e dei pantaloni gialli.

However, if the last noun you mention is feminine, you can choose to use either a masculine adjective or a feminine one.

Examples:

a. Ho comprato dei pantaloni e due <u>maglie</u> gialle.
b. Ho comprato dei pantaloni e due <u>maglie</u> gialli.

7.3 - Interrogative adjectives

Interrogative adjectives are words that modify a noun and ask a question.

These adjectives in Italian are placed before nouns and they can indicate a quantity, a quality, or an identity.

7.3.1 - Quantity

Quanto

It's used with masculine singular nouns.

Ex: Quanto zucchero vuoi nel caffè? -> How much sugar do you want in your coffee?

Quanta

It's used with feminine singular nouns.

Ex: Quanta farina ti serve? -> How much flour do you need?

Quanti

It's used with masculine plural nouns.

Ex: Quanti fratelli hai? -> How many brothers do you have?

Quante

It's used with feminine plural nouns.

Ex: Quante persone vengono alla festa? -> How many people will come to the party?

7.3.2 - Quality or identity

Che

It's used with both plural and singular, and masculine and feminine nouns. It has the same meaning as quale.

Ex: In che città sei nato? -> In which city were you bron?

Quale

It's used with masculine and feminine singular nouns

Ex: In quale ristorante vuoi andare? -> In which restaurant do you want to go?

Quali

It's used with masculine and feminine plural nouns

Ex: Quali pantaloni preferisci? -> Which pants do you prefer?

7.4 - Demonstrative adjectives

They indicate the object or the person a speaker refers to.

They are always placed before the noun they refer to and agree in gender and number with the noun they refer to.

Demonstrative adjectives can refer to near objects or to distant objects.

7.4.1 - Near objects

MASCULINE SINGULAR

For masculine singular nouns near you, you can use:

Questo + words starting with a **consonant**

Quest' + words starting with a **vowel or h**

Examples:

Questo cane -> This dog

Quest'elefante -> This elephant

FEMININE SINGULAR

For feminine singular nouns near you, you can use:

Questa + words starting with a **consonant**

Quest' + words starting with a **vowel or h**

Examples:

Questa pera -> This pear

Quest'amica -> This friend

MASCULINE PLURAL

For masculine plural nouns near you, you can use:

Questi + every plural masculine word

Examples:

Questi cani -> These dogs

Questi elefanti -> These elephants

FEMININE PLURAL

For feminine plural nouns near you, you can use:

Queste + every plural feminine word

Examples:

Queste pere -> These pears

Queste amiche -> These friends

7.4.2 - Distant objects

MASCULINE SINGULAR

For masculine singular nouns far from you, you can use:

Quello + words starting with **z, gn, ps, pn, x, s + consonant**, and **y/j/i + vowel**.

Quell' + words starting with a **vowel or h**

Quel + **with every other word**

Examples:

Quello scoiattolo -> That squirrel

Quell'elefante -> That elephant

Quel cane -> That dog

FEMININE SINGULAR

For feminine singular nouns far from you, you can use:

Quella + words starting with a **consonant**

Quell' + words starting with a **vowel or h**

Examples:

Quella pera -> That pear

Quell'amica -> That friend

MASCULINE PLURAL

For masculine plural nouns far from you, you can use:

Quegli + words starting with **z**, **gn**, **ps**, **pn**, **x**, **s + consonant**, and **y/j/i + vowel**; and with words starting with a vowel.

Quei + **with every other word**

Examples:

Quegli scoiattoli -> Those squirrels

Quegli elefanti -> Those elephants

Quei cani -> Those dogs

FEMININE PLURAL

For feminine plural nouns far from you, you can use:

Quelle + every plural feminine word

Examples:

Quelle pere -> Those pears
Quelle amiche -> Those friends

7.4.3 – Recap

INDICATES SOMETHING/SOMEONE NEAR THE SPEAKER

Masculine singular: Questo, quest'
Feminine singular: Questa, quest'
Masculine plural: Questi
Feminine plural: Queste

INDICATES SOMETHING/SOMEONE THAT'S FAR AWAY FROM THE SPEAKER

Masculine singular: Quello, quell, quell'
Feminine singular: Quella, quell'
Masculine plural: Quei, quegli
Feminine plural: Quelle

7.5 - Possessive adjectives

In Italian possessive adjectives are used to indicate ownership of something or relationship to someone.

Italian possessive adjectives are always used with the nouns they refer to.

Examples:

a. Questa non è la **tua** borsa (ownership)
This isn't your purse

b. Lei è **mia** sorella (relationship)
She's my sister

With the exception of the third person plural, which is always the same, possessive adjectives agree in gender and number with the noun they refer to.

PERSONAL PRONOUNS	MASCULINE SINGULAR POSSESSIVES	MASCULINE PLURAL POSSESSIVES
Io	Mio	Miei
Tu	Tuo	Tuoi
Lui	Suo	Suoi
Lei	Suo	Suoi
Noi	Nostro	Nostri
Voi	Vostro	Vostri
Loro	Loro	Loro

PERSONAL PRONOUNS	FEMININE SINGULAR POSSESSIVES	FEMININE PLURAL POSSESSIVES
Io	Mia	Mie
Tu	Tua	Tue
Lui	Sua	Sue
Lei	Sua	Sue
Noi	Nostra	Nostre
Voi	Vostra	Vostre
Loro	Loro	Loro

In Italian possessive adjectives are generally preceded by a definite article.

Examples:

La loro casa sta andando a fuoco
Their house is burning

Le sue scarpe costano 1500 €
Her/his shoes cost 1500 €

However, possessive adjectives aren't preceded by an article when:

a- They are placed before <u>singular nouns</u> expressing relationships – i.e. **padre, madre, figlio, figlia, marito, moglie, sorella, fratello, zio, zia, cognato, cognata** etc. – <u>without any other adjective between them.</u>
The only exceptions to this rule are the words *figliolo, figliola, babbo*. Indeed, they need an article before possessive adjectives.

Examples:

Mio padre si chiama Giuseppe

My father's name is Giuseppe

<u>Il</u> **mio** babbo si chiama Giuseppe

My daddy's name is Giuseppe

b- They are already preceded by a preposition

Ex: Quello è il cappotto <u>di</u> **mia** madre

That is my mother's coat

POSITION

Possessive adjectives generally precede the noun they refer to:

Ex: Questo è il mio libro di matematica

This is my math book

However, they can also follow the noun they refer to if the speaker wants to express some emphasis:

Ex: Questo libro di matematica è mio

This math book is mine

7.6 - Indefinite adjectives

They modify nouns indicating an unclear quantity. They agree in gender and number with the noun they replace or refer to.

7.6.1 - *Alcuno, certo, vario, diverso*

Alcuno, *certo*, *vario,* and *diverso* agree in gender and number with the noun they refer to.

Alcuno, *certo*, *vario,* and *diverso* indicate an indefinite amount of things or people.

Ex: **Alcune/Certe/Varie/Diverse** persone pensano che mangiare carne sia sbagliato

Some people believe that eating meat is wrong

7.6.2 - *Altro*

Altro agrees in gender and number with the noun it refers to.

Altro has different functions:

1. It is used to indicate another object or person, different from the one the speaker is talking about in a specific moment.

Ex: Ne parleremo in un **altro** momento

We'll talk about this another time/in another moment

2. It is used to indicate an object or person that is added in the moment one's speaking.

Ex: Posso avere un **altro** caffè, per favore?

Can I have one more coffee, please?

3. It is used to indicate the remaining objects or people from a group.

Ex: Le **altre** lenzuola sono ancora nella lavatrice

POSITION

Possessive adjectives generally precede the noun they refer to:

Ex: Questo è il mio libro di matematica

This is my math book

However, they can also follow the noun they refer to if the speaker wants to express some emphasis:

Ex: Questo libro di matematica è mio

This math book is mine

7.6 - Indefinite adjectives

They modify nouns indicating an unclear quantity. They agree in gender and number with the noun they replace or refer to.

7.6.1 - *Alcuno, certo, vario, diverso*

Alcuno, certo, vario, and *diverso* agree in gender and number with the noun they refer to.

Alcuno, certo, vario, and *diverso* indicate an indefinite amount of things or people.

Ex: **Alcune/Certe/Varie/Diverse** persone pensano che mangiare carne sia sbagliato
Some people believe that eating meat is wrong

7.6.2 - *Altro*

Altro agrees in gender and number with the noun it refers to.

Altro has different functions:

1. It is used to indicate another object or person, different from the one the speaker is talking about in a specific moment.

Ex: Ne parleremo in un **altro** momento
We'll talk about this another time/in another moment

2. It is used to indicate an object or person that is added in the moment one's speaking.

Ex: Posso avere un **altro** caffè, per favore?
Can I have one more coffee, please?

3. It is used to indicate the remaining objects or people from a group.

Ex: Le **altre** lenzuola sono ancora nella lavatrice

The other bed sheets are still in the washing machine

4. It is used to indicate a previous period of time compared to the actual one.

Ex: L'**altra** settimana ho incontrato Anna
Last week I met Anna

5. It's used to indicate that something is different compared to usual.

Ex: Oggi hai tutto un **altro** atteggiamento
Today you've got a whole new behavior

7.6.3 - *Molto*

Molto agrees in gender and number with the noun it refers to.

Molto is used to indicate a large number of objects or people.

Ex: **Molte** persone pensano che mangiare carne sia sbagliato
Many people believe that eating meat is wrong

7.6.4 - *Nessuno*

Nessuno is used only in the singular form – nessuno, nessuna.

In Italian, when *nessuno* is placed before a noun, it emphasizes the negation.

Ex 1: Anna non ha **nessun** amico
Anna has no friends

Ex 2: Non ho **nessuna** voglia di andare in palestra
I don't want to go to the gym

7.6.5 - *Ogni*

Ogni is invariabile and it's used only with singular nouns. It's used to indicate all the people or objects in a group.

Ex: Ringrazio Dio **ogni** giorno
I thank God every day

7.6.6 - *Parecchio*

Parecchio agrees in gender and number with the noun it refers to.

Parecchio is used to indicate a large number of objects or people. In Italian it has the exact same meaning of molto and tanto.

Ex: Ci sono **parecchie** persone qui
There are many/a lot of people here

7.6.7 - *Poco*

Poco can be translated as few or little. It agrees in gender and number with the noun it refers to.

Poco is used to indicate that there are a small number of things or people.

Ex 1: Mi fido solo di **poche** persone
I trust only a few people

Ex 2: Adesso ho **poco** tempo, parliamo più tardi
I've little time now; let's talk later

7.6.8 - *Qualche*

Qualche in Italian is invariable and it's used only with singular nouns.

It is used to indicate an amount of something, or an indefinite number of people or things.

Ex 1: Puoi darmi **qualche** consiglio?
Could you give me some advice?

Ex 2: Voglio passare **qualche** giorno a Parigi

I want to spend some days in Paris

7.6.9 - *Qualsiasi*

Qualsiasi is invariable and is used only with singular nouns.

Qualsiasi indicates any object or person, no matter which. It stresses the fact that any person or object you "choose" is okay.

Ex: **Qualsiasi** vestito sta bene su di te
Any dress looks good on you

7.6.10 - *Qualunque*

Qualunque is invariable in Italian and it is used only with singular nouns.

It indicates any object or person, no matter which. Also *qualunque* stresses the fact that any person or object you "choose" is okay. *Qualunque* and *qualsiasi* have the same meaning in Italian, and they're usually interchangeable.

Ex: Per **qualunque** dubbio, contattatemi
If you have any doubt, contact me

7.6.11 - Tale

Tale is invariable in Italian, and it is used only with singular nouns. It's used to add some emphasis.

Ex: E' stata una tale delusione!
It was such a disappointment!

7.6.12 - Tanto

Tanto agrees in gender and number with the noun it refers to.

Tanto has the same function of *molto*, and in Italian *tanto* and *molto* are basically intercheangable. *Tanto* is also used to indicate a large number of objects or people.

Ex: Tante persone pensano che mangiare carne sia sbagliato
Many people believe that eating meat is wrong

7.6.13 - Troppo

Troppo is used both in the singular and in the plural.

Troppo is used to indicate an excessive number of people or objects – usually a number that is more than it is acceptable.

Ex: Sono ancora **troppe** le persone che fumano

There are still too many people who smoke

7.6.14 - *Tutto*

Tutto agrees in gender and number with the noun it refers to.

Tutto is used to indicate all objects or all people.

Ex: **Tutti** i nostri amici sono francesi

All our friends are French

Chapter 8

Pronouns

8.1 - Personal subject pronouns

Italian personal subject pronouns are:

Io -> I

Tu -> you

Lui -> he

Lei -> she

Noi -> we

Voi -> you

Loro -> they

Examples:

a. **Io** sono Lucia

I'm Lucia

b. **Lei** è Maria

She's Maria

c. **Lui** è Stefano

He's Stefano

d. **Noi** siamo Riccardo e Ernesta

We're Riccardo and Ernesta

In Italian there's also a personal pronoun for objects and animals – *esso* for masculine nouns and *essa* for feminine nouns – but it is not generally used. You can find it in literature and in formal language.

USE AND POSITION

Personal pronouns in Italian can be omitted, since verbal forms usually change according to the person.

However, when personal pronouns are used, they usually precede the verb.

Example:

Ieri (io) ho comprato una macchina nuova -> Yesterday I bought a new car

Although personal pronouns can be omitted in Italian, they have to be used in the following cases:

- After conjunctions like *almeno (at least)*, *nemmeno (not even, either)*, *anche (too/also)*, *neanche (not even/neither, either)*, *pure (too/also)*, etc.

    Example: Neanche **io** ho letto il libro
    I haven't read the book either

- When they're used together with another subject.

    Example: **Io** e Marco andiamo al cinema
    Marco and I are going to the movies

- When in a sentence there are different verbs with different subjects.

    Example: **Io** cucino, **tu** apparecchi e **lei** lava i piatti
    I cook, you set the table, and she does the dishes

- When you want to express emphasis or contrast.

    Example: **Io** lavoro, **tu**, invece, non fai mai niente!
    I work, you, instead, always do nothing!

8.1.1 - Personal subject pronouns - the courtesy form

The courtesy form is a form used to address people in formal situations.

When we want to address people we do not know, people we've just met, people with a rank higher than ours, older people, etc., in Italian we generally use the courtesy form.

To do so, Italians use the third singular person Lei – in this case capitalized – to address both women and men.

Examples:

a. **Lei** è la Signora Rossi?

Are you Miss Rossi?

b. **Lei** è il Signor Rossi?

Are you Mr. Rossi?

The formal form Lei is only used with singular nouns. To address more than one person formally, in Italian we use the form **voi** both for women and men.

Example:

Voi siete i Signori Rossi?
Are you Mr. and Miss Rossi?

8.2 - Personal object pronouns

In Italian personal object pronouns can replace both direct and indirect objects.

Direct and indirect objects are the persons or things that receive the action of the verb.

The difference is that direct objects answer the questions "Who?" "What?".

Ex: Scrivo **un libro**
I write a book

What am I writing? Un libro. So "un libro" is a direct object.

Instead, indirect objects answer the questions "a chi?" - "to whom?" "for whom?".

Ex: Porto un libro **ad Anna**

I'm bringing a book to Anna

To whom am I bringing a book? Ad Anna. So "ad Anna" is an indirect object.

Italian personal object pronouns can have either a tonic or an atonic form.

8.2.1 - *Tonic personal pronouns replacing direct objects*

They can be placed both before and after the verb.
They answer the question "who?" "what?".
They're used to add more emphasis to what you're saying.

SUBJECT	TONIC PERSONAL PRONOUNS
Io	me
Tu	te
Lui	lui
Lei	lei
Noi	noi
Voi	voi
Loro	loro

Let's see an example:

Ex: Cercano Anna, non te
They're searching for Anna, not for you

Who are they searching for? Anna.

In this case Anna is the direct object that can be replaced by a tonic personal object pronoun.

Looking at the table above, since *Anna* is feminine singular, the pronoun we choose is lei. So, the sentence can be rewritten in this way:

Ex: Cercano lei, non te; Lei cercano, non te
It's she they're searching for, not you

8.2.2 - *Tonic personal pronouns replacing indirect objects*

They can be placed after or before the verb and answer the question "a chi?" - "to whom?" "for whom?".

SUBJECT	TONIC PERSONAL PRONOUNS
Io	a me
Tu	a te
Lui	a lui
Lei	a lei
Noi	a noi
Voi	a voi
Loro	a loro

Let's see an example:

Ex: Marco ha dato a Lucia un CD

Marco gave Lucia a CD

To whom Marco gave a CD? To Lucia.

In this case a Lucia is the indirect object that can be replaced by a tonic personal object pronoun.

Looking at the table above, since *Lucia* is feminine singular, the pronoun we choose is lei. So, the sentence can be rewritten in this way:

Marco ha dato **a lei** un CD; **A lei**, Marco ha dato un CD

Marco gave a cd to her

8.2.3 - Atonic personal pronouns replacing direct objects

They are placed before the verb and answer the question "who?" "what?".

SUBJECT	ATONIC PERSONAL PRONOUNS
Io	mi
Tu	ti
Lui	lo, l'
Lei	la, l'
Noi	ci
Voi	vi
Loro (masculine)	li
Loro (feminine)	le

Ex: Paolo è sempre in viaggio e io non vedo mai Paolo

Paolo is always traveling and I can never see Paolo

Who can I never see? Paolo

So, in this case Paolo is the direct object that can be replaced by an atonic personal object pronoun.

Looking at the table above, since *Paolo* is masculine singular and starts with a consonant, the pronoun we choose is lo. So, the sentence can be rewritten in this way:

Ex: Paolo è sempre in viaggio e io non lo vedo mai
Paolo is always traveling and I can never see him

8.2.4 - Atonic personal pronouns replacing indirect objects

They are all placed before the verb – except loro that is placed after the verb.
They answer the question " a chi?" - "to whom?" "for whom?".

SUBJECT	ATONIC PERSONAL PRONOUNS
Io	mi
Tu	ti
Lui	gli
Lei	le
Noi	ci
Voi	vi
Loro	gli/loro

Let's see an example:

Ex: Marco ha portato un regalo a Stefano e Matteo

Marco brought a gift to Stefano and Matteo

To whom did Marco bring a gift? To Stefano and Matteo

So, in this case *a Stefano and Matteo* is the indirect object that can be replaced by an atonic personal object pronoun.

Looking at the table above, since Stefano and Matteo are plural, the pronoun we choose is either gli or loro. So, the sentence can be rewritten in this way:

Ex: Marco **gli** ha portato un regalo

Marco brought them a gift

Ex: Marco ha portato **loro** un regalo

Marco brought them a gift

8.3 - Possessive pronouns

In Italian possessive pronouns are used to indicate ownership. Their form is the same as that of possessive adjectives. The only difference lies in their use. Indeed, adjectives are used with the nouns they refer to, while pronouns replace nouns.

Ex: Questa non è la **tua** borsa, è la **mia**

This isn't your purse; this is mine

In the example above, **tua** is an adjective since it comes before a noun, *borsa*. **Mia**, instead, is a pronoun, since it replaces a noun, *borsa*.

With the exception of the third person plural, that's always the same, possessive pronouns agree in gender and number with the noun they refer to.

PERSONAL PRONOUNS	**MASCULINE SINGULAR POSSESSIVES**	**MASCULINE PLURAL POSSESSIVES**
Io	Mio	Miei
Tu	Tuo	Tuoi
Lui	Suo	Suoi
Lei	Suo	Suoi
Noi	Nostro	Nostri
Voi	Vostro	Vostri
Loro	Loro	Loro

PERSONAL PRONOUNS	FEMININE SINGULAR POSSESSIVES	FEMININE PLURAL POSSESSIVES
Io	Mia	Mie
Tu	Tua	Tue
Lui	Sua	Sue
Lei	Sua	Sue
Noi	Nostra	Nostre
Voi	Vostra	Vostre
Loro	Loro	Loro

Possessive pronouns are always preceded either by an article or a preposition.

Examples:

a. Questi sono i tuoi regali, e quelli i suoi

These are your gifts and those are his/hers

b. Abbiamo già parlato del tuo matrimonio. Adesso parliamo del mio!

We have already talked about your wedding. Now let's talk about mine!

8.4 - Interrogative pronouns

Interrogative pronouns replace a noun and are used to ask a question.

Interrogative pronouns are chi, che, che cosa, cosa, quale, quanto.

8.4.1 - Chi

It's invariabile, so it doesn't change according to the gender or number of the noun it replaces.
It's used to ask questions about people.

Examples:

Chi siete?
Who are you?

Chi ha mangiato la mia torta?
Who ate my cake?

8.4.2 - Che/che cosa/cosa

They are invariable and they are used to ask questions about things.

Examples:

Che volete?

What do you want?

Che cosa volete?

What do you want?

Cosa volete?

What do you want?

8.4.3 - Quale/i – qual

They are used to ask questions about both people and things. Qual is used before words starting with a vowel.

Examples:

a. Ci sono solo due tipi di birre. **Quale** (birra) vuoi?

There are two types of beers. Which one do you want?

b. Ci sono due cellulari qui. **Qual** (cellulare) è il tuo?

There are two cell phones here. Which one is yours?

8.4.4 - *Quanto/a/i/e*

They are used to ask questions about both people and things.

Ex: Ho comprato queste pastiglie in farmacia. **Quante** (pastiglie) ne devo prendere al giorno?
I've bought these pills at the pharmacy. How many should I take per day

8.5 - Indefinite pronouns

Indefinite pronouns replace nouns and indicate an unclear quantity. They agree in gender and number with the noun they replace or refer to.

8.5.1 - *Alcuno, certo*

Alcuno and *certo* agree in gender and number with the noun they refer to.

Both *alcuno* and *certo* indicate an indefinite number of people or things.

Ex: **Alcuni/Certi** non verranno di sicuro
Some people surely won't come

8.5.2 - Altro

Altro agrees in gender and number with the noun it refers to.

Altro is usually used to indicate either an additional object or person, or a different object or person.

Ex: Questo cacciavite è rotto, passame un **altro**
This screwdriver is broken. Hand me another one

8.5.3 - Chiunque

Chiunque is invariable and it is used only with singular nouns. It means any person.

Ex: **Chiunque** voglia contattarci potrà farlo a questo numero
Anyone who wants to contact us can call this number

8.5.4 - Ciascuno, ognuno

Ciascuno and *ognuno* are invariable and they are used only with singular nouns – *ciascuno, ciascuna, ognuno, ognuna*.

Both *ciascuno* and *ognuno* mean each person.

Ex: Daremo una caramella a **ciascuno/ognuno**

We'll give each one a candy

8.5.5 - Molto

Molto agrees in gender and number with the noun it refers to.

Molto is used to indicate a large number of objects or people.

Ex: Questo quadro mi piace **molto**

I like this painting very much

8.5.6 - Nessuno

Nessuno is used only in the singular form and means nobody – nessuno, nessuna.

Ex: Io non vedo **nessuno**

I can see nobody

8.5.7 - Niente

Niente is invariabile and means nothing.

Ex: Non ho **niente** da nascondere

I've got nothing to hide

8.5.8 - Nulla

Nulla is invariable and means nothing. *Nulla* and *niente* are usually interchangeable in Italian.

Ex: Non ho **nulla** da nascondere
I've got nothing to hide

8.5.9 - Parecchio

Parecchio agrees in gender and number with the noun it refers to.

Parecchio is used to indicate a large number of objects or people. In Italian it has the exact same meaning of *molto* and *tanto*.

Ex: Questa macchina costa **parecchio**
This car costs a lot

8.5.10 - Poco

Poco agrees in gender and number with the noun it refers to.

Poco is used to indicate a small number of things or people.

Ex: A me servono almeno 100 grammi di farina, questa è **poca**
I need at least 100 grams of flour. This isn't enough

Ex: In **pochi** mi chiedono la fattura
Few people ask me for an invoice

8.5.11 - Qualcosa

Qualcosa is invariable and it is used only with singular nouns.

It's used to indicate a particular thing, when you do not know what this thing exaclty is.

Ex: C'è **qualcosa** che non va
Something is wrong

8.5.12 - Qualcuno

Qualcuno is invariable and it indicates a person. Usually, you do not know the identity of this person or you do not want to reveal the identity of this person.

Ex: **Qualcuno** ha lasciato queste rose per te
Someone left these roses for you

8.5.13 - Tanto

Tanto agrees in gender and number with the noun it refers to.

Tanto has the same function of *molto* and *parecchio*, and in Italian they're basically interchangeable. So tanto is also used to indicate a large number of objects or people.

Ex: Questo quadro mi piace **tanto**
I like this painting a lot

8.5.14 - Troppo

Troppo agrees in gender and number with the noun it refers to.

Troppo is used to indicate an excessive number of people or objects – usually a number that is more than what it is acceptable.

Ex: Questa pasta è **troppa** per me
This pasta is too much for me

8.5.15 - Tutto

Tutto agrees in gender and number with the noun it refers to.

Tutto is used to indicate all objects or all people.

Ex: Adesso pulisci **tutto**!
Now you clean everything up!

8.5.16 - Uno

Uno is invariable in Italian and it is used only with singular nouns. It means a person.

Ex: Ho visto **uno** che somigliava a tuo fratello
I saw a person who looked like your brother

8.5.17 - Vario, diverso

Vario and *diverso* agree in gender and number with the noun they refer to.

Both *vario* and *diverso* indicate an indefinite amount of things or people.

Ex: **Vari/diversi** hanno sostenuto di non sapere niente
Many people said they knew nothing

Chapter 9
Adverbs

Adverbs are invariable words whose function is to modify or specify the meaning of verbs, adjectives, nouns, other adverbs, or entire sentences.

Examples:

a. Dobbiamo finire questo compito *velocemente* -> We need to finish this task quickly.
b. Sono *molto* stanco. Lasciatemi in pace -> I'm very tired. Leave me alone.
c. Abbiamo comprato *poco* pane perché domani partiamo -> We haven't bought much bread because we're leaving tomorrow.
d. *Sinceramente*, mi dispiace per te -> Honestly, I feel sorry for you.

9.1 - Formation

In Italian the majority of adverbs is mainly formed by adding the suffix -mente to the feminine singular form of an adjective.

Examples

Rapido -> Rapida -> Rapida**mente** (quickly)
Sincero -> Sincera -> Sincera**mente** (honestly)

If the adjective ends in -le -lo or -re -ro, the final -e is dropped before adding the suffix -**mente**.

Examples
Genti**le** -> gentile -> gentil**mente** (kindly)
Regola**re** -> regolare -> regolar**mente** (regularly)

If the adjective ends in *-e* – and it is not preceded by *l* or *r* – it remains unchanged and only adds the suffix *-mente.*

Ex: Veloce -> veloce**mente** (fast)
Semplice -> semplice**mente** (easily)

However, not all the Italian adverbs are formed by adding the suffix -mente to an adjective – see paragraph 9.2.1.

9.2 - Types of adverbs in italian

In Italian there are many types of adverbs, each with a specific function: adverbs of manner, adverbs of place, adverbs of time, adverbs of degree, adverbs of quantity, interrogative adverbs.

9.2.1 - Adverbs of manner

They indicate the way in which an event happens.

Some examples are:

Bene, male, in un batter d'occhio, faccia a faccia, velocemente, lentamente, ingiustamente, dolcemente, di corsa, pesantemente, volentieri, alla svelta, corpo a corpo, così, sinceramente, amaramente, ripetutamente, attentamente, facilmente...

Ex: E' successo tutto molto *velocemente*
It all happened very fast

FORMATION

You can usually create adverbs of manner either by adding the suffix *–mente* or *–oni*.

- For the suffix *-mente* see paragraph 9.1.
- The suffix *–oni* is used only in a very few cases. The most common adverbs in *-oni* are: carponi, tentoni, ciondoloni, cavalcioni, penzoloni.

9.2.2 - Adverbs of place

They indicate the place where an event happens or the position of someone or something.

Some examples are:

Qui, qua, lì, là, dentro, fuori, intorno, giù, davanti, dietro, altrove, nei dintorni, dappertutto, ci, vi, ne, su, sopra, sotto, laggiù, lassù, ovunque, accanto...

Ex: L'ho cercato *dappertutto* ma non lo trovo
I searched for him everywhere but I can't find him

9.2.3 - Adverbs of time

They indicate the moment when an even takes place.

Some examples are:

Ormai, ora, presto, ancora, domani, subito, prima, dopo, ieri, oggi, di buon ora, mai, sempre, spesso, adesso, dopodomani, precedentemente, poi, allora, successivamente, di tanto in tanto...

Ex: Non è *ancora* arrivato?

Isn't he here yet?

9.2.4 - Adverbs of degree

They express an opinion or judgment about something or someone in the form of:

AFFIRMATION

Purtroppo, giustamente, ingiustamente, sfortunatamente, fortunatamente, stranamente, sicuramente, certo, per l'appunto, di certo, sì, sicuro, certamente, ovviamente, esatto…

Ex: *Sfortunatamente*, Giulia aveva ragione
Unfortunately, Giulia was right

NEGATION

No, non, neanche per idea, nemmeno per sogno, neanche per sogno, mai, né, neanche, affatto, neppure…

Ex: Non ci ha *neanche* ringraziati
He didn't even thank us

The adverb *non* is always placed before verbs and it can be used with the adverbs *mica*, *affatto*, *proprio*, to strengthen the negation.

Examples:

Non sono *mica* stato io -> It wasn't me

Non sono *affatto* d'accordo -> I totally disagree

Non capisco *proprio* le tue ragioni -> I can't really understand your point

When *mica* is used with *non*, it can replace *non* in the sentence.

Examples:

Mica sono stato io! -> It wasn't me!

DOUBT

Probabilmente, eventualmente, se, chissà, semmai, nell'eventualità, forse, magari, quasi, nel caso...

Ex: Non è ancora arrivato. *Magari* è bloccato nel traffico
He hasn't arrived yet. Maybe he's stuck in the traffic jam

9.2.5 - Adverbs of quantity

They indicate an unspecified amount of something.

Some examples are:

Poco, molto, meno, parecchio, abbastanza, quasi, nè più nè meno, tanto più, appena, troppo, niente, nulla...

Ex: Ha studiato *parecchio* per quest'esame
He studied hard for this exam

9.2.6 - Interrogative adverbs

They are used to ask a question.

>Quando   Dove   Come
>Quanto   Perché/Come mai

They can indicate:

TIME
Quando?

Ex: *Quando* arrivano?
When will they arrive?

PLACE
Dove?

Ex: *Dove* sono?

Where am I?

MANNER

Come?

Ex: *Com*'è andato il volo?
How was your flight?

QUANTITY

Quanto?

Ex: *Quanto* costa?
How much is it?

CAUSE

Perché? – Come mai?

Ex: *Perché/come mai* non siete venuti?
Why didn't you come?

Mai can also emphasize *perché*.

Ex: *Perché mai* faresti una cosa del genere?
Why on earth would you do such a thing?

Interrogative adverbs are used both in direct and indirect questions

Examples:

a. *Quanto* costa? (direct)
How much is it?

b. *Quando* arriva tua sorella? (direct)
When will your sister arrive?

c. Dimmi *dove* posso trovarlo (indirect)
Tell me where I can find him

d. Non so *perché* è arrabbiato con me (indirect)
I don't know why he's angry with me

9.3 - The position of adverbs

Generally, the position of adverbs can be fixed or, on the contrary, can vary.

You can learn how to correctly use adverbs through practice.

- Adverbs of manner do not have a fixed position.

Examples:

a. Taglia, **lentamente**, in questo punto

Cut, slowly, in this point

b. **Lentamente**, taglia in questo punto

Slowly, cut in this point

c. Taglia in questo punto, **lentamente**

Cut in this point, slowly

- If an adverb refers to a verb, it is placed after the verb.

Ex: Martina <u>parla</u> **poco**

Martina doesn't talk much

- If the adverb refers to an adjective or a noun, it is placed before the adjective or the noun.

Examples:

Oggi sono **molto** <u>soddisfatta</u> di quello che ho dipinto

I'm very proud of what I've painted today

Compra **tante** <u>bibite</u>. Domani è il compleanno di Rita

Buy a lot of drinks. Tomorrow is Rita's birthday

- If the adverb refers to a sentence, it does not have a fixed position.

Examples:

Sinceramente, mi dispiace per te

Honestly, I feel sorry for you

Mi dispiace per te, **sinceramente**

I feel sorry for you, honestly

In some cases, both the position of an adverb, intonation, punctuation, and pauses can change the meaning of a sentence.

Examples:

a. Io capisco **solamente** l'italiano

I understand only Italian

b. **Solamente** io capisco l'italiano

I'm the only one who can understand Italian

c. Hai fatto tutto **bene**

You've done everything right

d. Hai fatto tutto, **bene**!

You've done everything, good!

Chapter 10
Prepositions

Prepositions are invariable words that can precede nouns, pronouns, or infinitives.

Italian prepositions are usually considered by students one of the most difficult Italian topics to learn.

The reason is that even if there are usually some rules that explain their usage, in many cases these rules do not apply. And prepositions are to be learned in context, by heart.

In Italian there are two types of prepositions: simple prepositions and contracted prepositions.

10.1 - Simple prepositions

The main simple prepositions are *di, a, da, in, con, su, per, tra/fra*.

USE

10.1.1 - Di

Di can be used to:

- Indicate possession

    Ex: Questa è la borsa di Marta
    This is Marta's bag

- Indicate the thing someone or something is full of or lacking in

    Ex: Ho la macchina piena di bottiglie
    My car is full of bottles

    Ex: Questo libro è privo di ironia
    This books lacks in irony

- Indicate a relationship

    Ex: Il tipo con la maglia verde è il fratello di Roberta
    The guy with the green t-shirt is Roberta's brother

- Indicate a topic about which someone discussed or is discussing

Ex: Ieri abbiamo parlato **di** economia

Yesterday we talked about economics

- Indicate someone's age

    Ex: Ho una sorella **di** 24 anni

    I have a sister of 24 years

- Indicate the material something is made of

    Ex: Questo è un maglione **di** lana merino

    This sweater is made of merino wool

- Indicate the crime someone is charged with

    Ex: Davide è accusato **di** furto con scasso

    Davide is charged with burglary

- Indicate the second term of comparison

    Ex: Massimo è più alto **di** Andrea

    Massimo is higher than Andrea

10.1.2 - A

A is typically used:

- To express place and it's normally used with names of towns and villages and cardinal points

    Ex: Abito a Londra
    I live in London

    Ex: Andiamo a nord
    We're going north

- After certain verbs like:

    Andare (to go)
    Venire (to come)
    Cominciare (to start/begin)
    Continuare (to continue)
    Riuscire (can/manage/to be able to)

    In this case, a is followed by a verb in the infinitive

    Ex: Vado a correre

I'm going for a run

Ex: Giulia continua **a** <u>ridere</u>
Giulia keeps laughing

- To express the price something is sold or bought:

    Ex: Ho venduto il mio computer **a** 1250 €
    I sold my computer for 1250 €

- To express the age when someone did/does something:

    Ex: Ho scalato l'Everest **a** 34 anni
    I climbed Everest when I was 34

10.1.3 - Da

Da can indicate:

- The origin of something or someone

    Ex: Alejandro viene **da** Madrid
    Alejandro comes from Madrid

- The value of something

Ex: E' una domanda **da** un milione di dollari

It's a one million dollar question

- The place where a person is going to or is staying at. It is especially used with proper names, family names, professions, or pronouns

Ex: Vado **da** Miriam

I go to Miriam's house

Ex: Starò **da** Miriam per una settimana

I'm staying at Miriam's house for a week

- Detachment from someone or something

Ex: Vado via **da** Milano

I'm leaving Milan

- The time when you start or started doing something

Ex: E' **da** due anni che vivo a Roma

I've been living in Rome for two years

- The construction indefinite pronouns + da + infinitive

Ex: Dammi qualcosa **da** mangiare, sto morendo di fame!

Give me something to eat; I'm starving!

- It is used with some verbs such as *escludere, difendersi, dipendere, ripararsi.*

    Ex: Io dipendo **da** te

    I depend on you

10.1.4 - *In*

In is typically used:

- To express place and it's normally used with names of regions and nations, and geographical areas

    Ex: Vado **in** Toscana

    I'm going to Tuscany

    Ex: Abito **in** Inghilterra

    I live in England

    Ex: Vado **in** montagna

    I'm going to the mountains

- With shops

    Ex: Vado **in** panetteria

    I'm going to the bakery

- With means of transport

    Ex: Vado a scuola **in** macchina

    I go to school by car

10.1.5 - Con

Con generally means *with* and can indicate:

- A relation of some kind

    Ex: Anna sta cenando **con** suo fratello

    Anna is having dinner with her brother

- The way you do an action

    Ex: Guarda **con** attenzione

    Look carefully

- The reason why you do the action expressed by the verb

    Ex: **Con** questo tempo gli aerei non partono

    In this weather flights won't leave the ground

10.1.6 - Su

Su can indicate:

- A topic

    Ex: Ho guardato un film **su** Martin L. King

    I watched a movie about Martin L. King

- On/over something; up, against, to

    Ex: Si sta arrampicando **su** un albero

    S/he's climbing a tree

10.1.7 - Per

Per can indicate:

- The place through which you pass/go through

    Ex: Passi **per** via Dante? No, faccio un'altra strada

Are you passing through via Dante? No, I'll pass through another road

- The person or thing to whom an advantage or disadvantage is brought

    Ex: Sto facendo gli straordinari solo **per** te!
    I'm doing overtime only for you

- The price something is sold or bought

    Ex: Ho comprato/venduto questa macchina **per** 15.000 €
    I bought/sold this car for 15.000 €

- The reason why a person has been sentenced

    Ex: E' stato condannato a 1 anno di carcere **per** furto
    He's been sentenced to 1 year imprisonment for theft

- A substitution of someone or something for another person/object

    Ex: Scusa, ti ho scambiato **per** un'altra persona!
    I'm sorry, I've mistaken you for another person

10.1.8 - Tra/fra

Tra and fra have the same functions and can indicate:

- A relation with someone or something

    Ex: Avanti, raccontami tutto, sei **tra** amici!
    Come on, tell me everything; you're among friends!

- The location of someone or something

    Ex: Giulio è quello **tra** Francesco e Sara
    Giulio is the one between Francesco and Sara

- A distance or a period of time

    Ex: **Tra** dieci minuti si mangia
    In ten minutes we eat

- An estimation of something – used with numbers

    Ex: E' alto **tra** 1.60 e 1.67
    He's between 1.60 and 1.67 meters tall

Ex: E' un uomo **tra** i 20 e i 30 anni

He's a man in his mid-to late 20s

- The group the thing or person you are talking about is part of

Ex: **Tra** tutti gli sport che ci sono dovevi scegliere proprio il rafting?

Among all the sports, you had to choose rafting?

10.2 - Contracted prepositions

Contracted prepositions agree in gender and number with the noun they refer to.

Contracted prepositions are formed of a simple preposition + an article.

	IL	**LO**	**L'**	**LA**
DI	Del	Dello	Dell'	Della
A	Al	Allo	All'	Alla
DA	Dal	Dallo	Dall'	Dalla
IN	Nel	Nello	Nell'	Nella
CON	Con il Col	Con lo Collo	Con l' Coll'	Con la Colla
SU	Sul	Sullo	Sull'	Sulla
PER	Per il	Per lo	Per l'	Per la
TRA	Tra il	Tra lo	Tra l'	Tra la
FRA	Fra il	Fra lo	Fra l'	Fra la

	I	GLI	LE
DI	Dei	Degli	Delle
A	Ai	Agli	Alle
DA	Dai	Dagli	Dalle
IN	Nei	Negli	Nelle
CON	Con i / Coi	Con gli / Cogli	Con le / Colle
SU	Sui	Sugli	Sulle
PER	Per i	Per gli	Per le
TRA	Tra i	Tra gli	Tra le
FRA	Fra i	Fra gli	Fra le

USE

Contracted prepositions usually have the same function of simple prepositions.

In addition to the uses listed in Paragraph 10.1, we're going to add these ones:

10.2.1 - Con

Con generally means *with* and can indicate:

- A quality or characteristic:

    Ex: Guarda che bello quel cucciolo **con** il fiocco rosso
    Look how lovely the puppy with the red bow is

- A means, thing, or person thanks to whom you can do something

    Ex: Vado a scuola **con** l'autobus
    I go to school by bus

10.2.2 - Su

Su can indicate:

- An approximate indication of age, price, or measure, time, etc.

    Ex: Ho visto il ladro! Era un uomo **sui** 30 anni…
    I saw the burglar! He was a man around 30 years old…

    Ex: Questa macchina fotografica costa **sui** 1000 €
    This camera costs around 1000 €

Ex: Matteo è molto magro, pesa **sui** 60 kg

Matteo is very slim. He weighs around 60 kg

10.3 - Simple prepositions or contracted prepositions?

It's often difficult for learners to understand when and how to use contracted prepositions and when and how to use simple prepositions.

The reason is that there isn't a precise rule on when and how to use one instead of the other.

It is only possible to say that:

Contracted prepositions are generally **not used**:

1. Before names of cities. Some exceptions are: L'Aquila, la Spezia, L'Avana, Il Cairo, La Mecca, La Valletta.

Examples:

a. Vado a Parigi

I go to Paris

b. Abito a <u>Madrid</u>

I live in Madrid

c. Vado al <u>Cairo</u>

I go to Cairo

2. Before personal names or surnames

Examples:

a. Vado da <u>Mario</u>

I go to Mario's home

b. Questo portafoglio è di <u>Luciana Rossi</u>

This wallet is Luciana Rossi's

3. Before indefinite articles

Examples:

a. Questo è un regalo **per** <u>un</u> mio amico

This is a gift for one of my friends

b. Mi sono iscritto a <u>un</u> corso di ballo

I signed up for dance class

4. Before an infinitive

Examples:

a. Luca è appena uscito. Se corri, forse, riesci **a** <u>raggiungerlo</u>
Luca has just gone out. If you run, maybe, you can catch him

b. Mi ha chiamata **per** <u>dirmi</u> che non sarebbe venuto alla festa
He called me to let me know he wouldn't have come to the party

5. With nouns indicating relationships – fratello, sorella, cugino, cugina, madre, padre, etc. – if they are singular or if they are preceded by possessive adjectives:

Ex: Vado **da** <u>mia sorella</u>
I'm going to my sister's house

6. In some expressions used as adverbs: *con gioia*, *per paura*, *a ragione*, *in sostanza*, etc.

7. In many expressions with the preposition da: *abito da sera, ferro da stiro, comportarsi da gentiluomo,* etc.

8. With the preposition di when it is followed by a material: *di ferro*, *di seta*, *di lana*, *di ottone*, etc.

Moreover, it is also possible to say that contracted prepositions **are** generally **used**:

1. Before nouns of regions, countries, continents, islands, seas, lakes, rivers, and mountains

Examples:

a. Domani vado in vacanza **sulle** Alpi
Tomorrow I'll go on vacation to the Alps

b. L'anno prossimo, vado a fare una crociera **sul** Mar Rosso
Next year I'm going on a cruise on the Red Sea

c. Lunedì i miei genitori tornano **dalla** Germania
On Monday my parents come back from Gemany

Often the preposition in is an exception to this rule. Indeed, Italians say "vivo in Argentina" and not "vivo nell'Argentina."

Ex: Vivo in Argentina
I live in Argentina

However, if the noun the preposition refers to is preceded or followed by an adjective or a complement that determines it, Italians use preopsizioni articolate.

Ex: Vivo **nella** bella Argentina
I live in beautiful Argentina

2. To form the plural of indefinite articles – un, uno, una

Examples:

a. Ci sono **delle** sedie in salotto
There are some chairs in the living room

b. Ci sono **dei** coltelli sul tavolo
There are some knives on the table

3. Before nouns indicating relationships – fratello, sorella, cugino, cugina, madre, padre, etc. – if they are plural and they are preceded by possessive adjectives.

Ex: Sto andando **dai** nostri genitori
I'm going to our parents' house

Chapter 11
Conjunctions

Conjunctions are invariable words used to join both words and clauses together.

In Italian there are two types of conjunctions: coordinating conjunctions and subordinating conjunctions.

Coordinating conjunctions connect two words or two sentences that are on the same level.

Ex: Anna è alta e bionda
Anna is tall and blond

Subordinating conjunctions, on the other hand, connect two sentences where one depends on the other – the dependent clause depends on the main clause.

Ex: **Dato che** nevicava, siamo rimasti a casa
Since it was snowing, we stayed home

In the example above, *siamo rimasti a casa* is the main clause, since it can be used alone. *Dato che nevicava*, is the dependent clause.

In Italian there are many coordinating and subordinating conjunctions. Let's look at the most common ones.

11.1 - Coordinating conjunctions

1. Conjunctions:

E (and) – *anche* (also) – *pure, perfino* (even) – *inoltre* (in addition to) – *ancora* (yet, again)

Function:

They present non-contrasting elements

Examples:

a. Carlo *e* Francesco sono amici

Carlo and Francesco are friends

b. Verrò *anch*'io alla festa

I'll come to the party too

c. *Perfino* io andrò alla festa! Devi venirci!

Even I'll go to the party! You have to come!

d. Francesco si è presentato alla festa senza essere stato invitato, *inoltre* si è comportato malissimo con Lucia.

Francesco showed up at the party without having been invited; besides, he was horrible to Lucia.

e. Stai *ancora* mangiando?

Are you still eating?

2. Conjunctions:

Nè (neither...nor) – *neanche, neppure, nemmeno* (not even, neither, either)

Function:

They present non-contrasting negative elements

Examples:

a. *Nè* te *nè* io siamo bravi in matematica

Neither you nor I are good in math

b. *Neanche/neppure/nemmeno* io sono brava in matematica

I'm not good at math either

3. Conjunctions:

O, oppure (otherwise, or)

Function:

They present an alternative element

Ex: Puoi comprare questo *o/oppure* quello

You can buy this or that

4. Conjunctions:

Ma (but, however) – *tuttavia, però* (however, nevertheless) – *eppure* (yet, but, still) – *anzi* (actually, on the contrary, rather) – *nonostante* (despite, in spite of, although, even though) – *bensì* (but) – *piuttosto* (rather, instead) – *invece* (but, instead) - *mentre* (while, whereas) – *ciò nonostante* (despite this)

Function:

They present a contrast or an exception

Examples:

a. Ho bussato *ma* non ha risposto nessuno

I knocked but no one answered

b. Era un esame difficile, *tuttavia/però* l'ha superato a pieni voti

It was a difficult exam; however, he passed it with flying colors

c. Era un esame difficile, *eppure* l'ha superato a pieni voti

It was a difficult exam; yet he passed it with flying colors

d. Non mi disturbi affatto, *anzi*

You don't bother me; actually it's quite the opposite

e. Carlo è uscito di casa *nonostante* la bufera

Carlo went out despite the blizzard

f. Non partiremo lunedì *bensì* sabato

We won't leave on Monday but on Saturday

g. No, niente caffè, grazie, *piuttosto* gradirei un bicchiere di vino

No, no coffee thanks; I'd rather have a glass of wine

h. Credevo fosse un amico, *invece* mi ha tradito

I thought he was a friend; instead he betrayed me

i. Continua a lamentarsi, *mentre* dovrebbe essere contento

He keeps complaining while he should be happy

l. Sapeva che era pericoloso *ciò nonostante* si è presentata all'appuntamento

She knew it was dangerous; despite this, she went on the date

5. Conjunctions:

Dunque (therefore, hence) – *perciò, quindi, pertanto, allora, per cui, così* (therefore, for this reason, so, hence, thus) – *insomma* (so, in short, in conclusion)

Function:
They present a conclusion

Examples:

a. Le luci erano spente, *dunque* non erano in casa

The lights were off; hence, they weren't home

b. Oggi c'erano i saldi, *perciò/quindi/pertanto/allora/per cui/così* ho deciso di comprare quattro gonne

Today there was a sale, so I decided to buy four skirts

c. L'auto era confortevole, affidabile e economica, *insomma* un vero affare!

The car was comfortable, reliable, and low-cost; in short a real bargain!

6. Conjunctions:

Infatti, difatti (in fact) – *cioè, ovvero, vale a dire* (that is to say)

Function:

They present an explanation that is linked to an affirmation that has just been said

Examples:

a. Fa freddo, *infatti/difatti* le strade sono ghiacciate

It's cold; in fact streets are icy

b. Arriverò martedì, *cioè/ovvero/vale a dire* il 30 di gennaio

I'll arrive on Tuesday; that's to say the 30th of January

7. Conjunctions:

E...e (both...and) – *o...o* (either...or) – *né...nè* (neither...nor) – *sia...sia* (both...and) – *non solo...ma anche* (not only...but also) – *tanto...quanto* (as much as) – *sia che...sia che* (whether...or)

Function:

They work in pairs to link together non-contrasting elements

Examples:

a. Ha perso *e* il portafoglio, *e* l'orologio

He lost both his wallet and his watch

b. Puoi comprare *o* questo *o* quello

You can buy either this or that

c. Non puoi comprare *né* questo *nè* quello

You can buy neither this nor that

d. Puoi comprare *sia* questo *sia* quello

You can buy both this and that

e. *Non solo* ha perso l'orologio *ma anche* il portafoglio

Not only did he lose his watch but also his wallet

f. *Sia che* tu mi regali un'auto *sia che* tu non me la regali, per me fa lo stesso

Whether you buy me a car or not, to me it's the same

11.2 - Subordinating conjunctions

1. Conjunctions:

Siccome, siccome che, poiché, dal momento che, dato che, visto che (given that, since) – *perché* (because, because of)

Function:

They present a reason, a cause

Examples:

a. *Siccome/poiché/dal momento che/dato che/visto che* **pioveva, non siamo andati in spiaggia**

Since it was raining, we didn't go to the beach

b. **Non sono venuto** *perché* **avevo la febbre**

I didn't come because I had a fever

2. Conjunctions:

Affinché, perché (in order that, so that)

Function:
They present a purpose

Ex: Sono severo con te *affinché/perché* tu possa imparare
I'm strict with you so that you can learn

3. Conjunctions:

Quando (when) – *finché, fin quando* (until) – *da quando* (since) – *dopo che* (after, after that) – *prima che* (before, before that) – *intanto che, mentre* (while) – *Non appena, appena* (as soon as) – *ogni volta che* (each time, every time) – *ora che, adesso che* (now that)

Function:

They refer to the time when something happens, and they indicate a sentence containing a temporal relationship

Examples:

a. *Quando* sono arrivato, non c'era nessuno in casa

When I got there, nobody was at home

b. Lo aspetteremo *finché/fin quando* non arriverà

We'll wait for him until he comes

c. *Da quando* hai preso la patente sei sempre felice

Since you got your driver's licence you're always happy

d. *Dopo che* avrai pulito la tua camera, potrai uscire

After you clean your room, you can go out

e. Presto, nascondilo *prima che arrivi*

Hurry, hide it before he gets here

f. *Intanto che/mentre io cucino, tu taglia il prato*

While I cook, you mow the lawn

g. *Non appena/appena* sarà qui, gli chiederemo delle spiegazioni

As soon as he gets here, we'll ask him to explain

h. *Ogni volta* che usciamo, mi offre un gelato

Every time we go out, he offers me an ice-cream

i. *Ora che/adesso che* abbiamo finito i compiti possiamo uscire

Now that we finished our homework, we can go out

4. Conjunctions:

Anche quando (even when) – *benché*, *sebbene* (although, even though, albeit, though) – *nonostante* (despite, in spite of, although, even though)

Function:

They present a concession

Examples:

a. Si scusa *anche quando* ha ragione

He's apologizes even when he's right

b. *Benché/sebbene* avesse ragione, si scusò

Even if he was right, he apologized

c. *Nonostante* ci fosse una tormenta, Carlo uscì di casa

Despite there being a blizzard, Carlo went out

5. Conjunctions:

Che (that) – *cioè, ovvero, vale a dire* (that's to say, namely) – *in altre parole* (in other words, that's to say)

Function:
They explain or complete what has been said in the main clause.

Examples:

a. E' possibile *che* io arrivi in ritardo

It's possible that I'll be late

b. Vado a coccolarmi, *cioè/ovvero/vale a dire* vado a mangiare un po' di cioccolato

I'm going to cuddle myself; that's to say I'm going to eat some chocolate

c. Vado a coccolarmi, *in altre parole* vado a mangiare un po' di cioccolato

I'm going to cuddle myself; in other words, I'm going to eat some chocolate

6. Conjunctions:

Se, qualora (if, in case) – *purchè, a condizione che, a patto che* (as long as, provided that)

Function:

They present a condition.

Examples:

a. *Se/qualora* arrivasse, ditemelo subito

If he arrives, tell me immediately

b. Ti racconterò la mia storia, *purché/a condizione che/a patto che* tu mi racconti la tua

I'll tell you my story provided that you tell me yours

7. Conjunctions:

Come (as, like) – *come se* (as if)

Function:

They present the way something happened.

Examples:

a. Ho fatto *come* mi è stato detto

I did as I was told

b. Si comportava *come se* avesse ragione quando, invece, aveva torto marcio

Che (that) – *cioè, ovvero, vale a dire* (that's to say, namely) – *in altre parole* (in other words, that's to say)

Function:
They explain or complete what has been said in the main clause.

Examples:

a. E' possibile *che* io arrivi in ritardo

It's possible that I'll be late

b. Vado a coccolarmi, *cioè/ovvero/vale a dire* vado a mangiare un po' di cioccolato

I'm going to cuddle myself; that's to say I'm going to eat some chocolate

c. Vado a coccolarmi, *in altre parole* vado a mangiare un po' di cioccolato

I'm going to cuddle myself; in other words, I'm going to eat some chocolate

6. Conjunctions:

Se, qualora (if, in case) – *purchè, a condizione che, a patto che* (as long as, provided that)

Function:

They present a condition.

Examples:

a. *Se/qualora* arrivasse, ditemelo subito

If he arrives, tell me immediately

b. Ti racconterò la mia storia, *purché/a condizione che/a patto che* tu mi racconti la tua

I'll tell you my story provided that you tell me yours

7. Conjunctions:

Come (as, like) – *come se* (as if)

Function:

They present the way something happened.

Examples:

a. Ho fatto *come* mi è stato detto

I did as I was told

b. Si comportava *come se* avesse ragione quando, invece, aveva torto marcio

He behaved as if he was right, when instead he was dead wrong

8. Conjunctions:

Mentre (while)

Function:

They present a contrast.

Examples:

a. Il libro è bello *mentre* il film è terribile

The book is good while the movie is terrible

9. Conjunctions:

Tranne che, eccetto che, salvo che (except) – *a meno che* (unless)

Function:

They present a limitation.

Examples:

a. Farò di tutto per farlo ragionare *tranne che/eccetto che/salvo che* implorarlo

I'll do whatever it takes to talk some sense into him except to implore him

b. Non esce mai di casa *a meno che* non ci sia un'emergenza

She never leaves her home unless there's an emergency

10. Conjunctions:

Se (if, whether) – *come* (how) – *quando* (when) – *quanto* (how much) – *perché* (why)

Function:

They present a sentence containing a question or a doubt.

Examples:

a. Non sapeva *se* presentarsi all'appuntamento oppure no

She didn't know whether to show up to her date or not

b. Mi chiedo *come* gli dirò la verità

I'm wondering how I'll tell him the truth

c. Mi chiedo *quando* mi dirà la verità

I'm wondering when he'll tell me the truth

d. Mi domando *quanto* gli sarà costato

I'm wondering how much it cost him

e. Mi chiese *perché* lo avessi fatto

He asked me why I did that

11. Conjunctions:

Come (like, as) – *più/meno...di* (more/less...than)

Function:

They present a comparison.

Examples:

a. Giada è alta *come* Luca

Giada is as tall as Luca

b. Marco è *più/meno* simpatico *di* quanto mi aspettassi

Marco is nicer/less nice than I expected

12. Conjunctions:

Il quale, la quale, i quali, le quali (who, that) – *che* (who, which, that)

Function:

They present a relative sentence.

Examples:

a. Giulia ha una cugina, *la quale* parla sette lingue

Giulia has a cousin who speaks seven languages

b. Ho visto un film *che* mi è piaciuto tantissomo

I saw a movie that I really liked

Chapter 12

There is and there are

In Italian there is and there are are formed with ci + verb essere.

C'è -> There is

Ci sono -> There are

C'è is used with singular nouns while ci sono is used with plural nouns.

Examples:

a. C'è un letto

There's a bed

b. Ci sono tre letti

There are three beds

NEGATIVE SENTENCE

In Italian the negative form of *c'è* and *ci sono* is formed by placing the word **non** before them.

Ex1: **Non** c'è

There isn't

Ex2: **Non** ci sono

There aren't

Examples:

a. Non **c'è** un letto qui

There isn't a bed here

b. Non **ci sono** tre letti here

There aren't three beds here

12.1 - Other meanings of c'e' and ci sono

In informal Italian, c'è and ci sono can have other meanings too. In fact, they can mean both *Have you understood?* or *Are you ready?*

Ex1: **Ci sei?** Il taxi è arrivato

Are you ready? The taxi's here

Ex2: Quindi, gli avverbi si usano per introdurre una domanda. **Ci siete** fino a qui?

Therefore, adverbs are used to introduce a question. Have you understood up until now?

Chapter 13

The comparative and the superlative

13.1 - The comparative

The comparative is a construction that allows comparison of two or more entities – verbs, nouns, pronouns, adjectives, or adverbs – expressing some degree of superiority, inferiority or equality.

The first entity is called *first term of comparison*, while the second is called *second term of comparison*.

Example:

(1st term of comparison) Mario è più alto *(2nd term of comparison)* di Giacomo

(1st term of comparison) Mario is taller *(2nd term of comparison)* than Giacomo

13.1.1 - *Expressing superiority*

In Italian the comparative of superiority can be formed in two ways.

FIRST WAY: *PIU'...DI*

The first way to express superiority in Italian is to use the word più (more) before an adjective and the word di (than) before the second term of comparison if this is <u>a noun and a pronoun (not preceded by a preposition) or an adverb</u>.

Examples:

a. Lucia è più intelligente di Angela
Lucia is smarter than Angela

b. Martina è più contenta di prima
Martina is happier than before

SECOND WAY: *PIU'...CHE*

The second way to form the comparative of superiority is to use the word più (more) before an adjective and the word che – than – before the second term of comparison if this is <u>a noun and a pronoun (preceded by a preposition) or when the aim is to compare two adjectives of quality or two infinitives</u>.

Examples:

a. Francesco è **più** bravo in matematica **che** in latino
Francesco is better at math than at Latin

b. Marco è **più** bello **che** intelligente
Marco is more beautiful than intelligent

c. Correre è **più** faticoso **che** camminare
Running is more tiring than walking

13.1.2 - *Expressing inferiority*

Also, the comparative of inferiority can be formed in two ways.

FIRST WAY: *MENO...DI*

The first way to express inferiority in Italian is to use the word **meno** (less) before an adjective and the word **di** (than) before the second term of comparison if this is <u>a noun and a pronoun (not preceded by a preposition) or an adverb</u>.

Examples:

a. Lucia è **meno** intelligente **di** Angela
Lucia is less intelligent than Angela

b. Martina è meno contenta di prima

Martina is less happy than before

SECOND WAY: *MENO...CHE*

The second way to form the comparative of inferiority is to use the word meno (less) before an adjective and the word che – than – before the second term of comparison if this is <u>a noun and a pronoun (preceded by a preposition) or when the aim is to compare two adjectives of quality or two infinitives</u>.

Examples:

a. Francesco è meno bravo in matematica che in latino

Francesco is worse at math than at Latin

b. Camminare è meno faticoso che correre

Walking is less tiring than running

13.1.3 - Expressing equality

The comparative of equality can be formed in two ways.

FIRST WAY: *TANTO...QUANTO*

To express equality, Italian uses tanto before an adjective and quanto before the 2nd term of comparison.

Ex: Nicola è **tanto** veloce **quanto** Paolo

Nicola is as fast as Paolo

SECOND WAY: ...*COME/QUANTO*

As we've just studied, the comparative of equality is formed by using **tanto** before an adjective and **quanto** before the 2nd term of comparison.

However, the word **tanto** can also be omitted. In this case, the second term of comparison can be preceded either by **quanto** or by **come**.

Ex: Francesca è magra **quanto/come** Sofia

Francesca is as slim as Sofia

13.1.4 - *Irregular comparative forms*

In Italian there are also some comparatives that are formed irregularly. In the table below, you'll find the most common ones.

ADJECTIVE OR ADVERB	COMPARATIVE
Buono (good)	**Migliore** (better)
Cattivo (bad)	**Peggiore** (worse)
Grande (big)	**Maggiore** (bigger)
Piccolo (small)	**Minore** (smaller)
Alto (high)	**Superiore** (higher)
Basso (low)	**Inferiore** (lower)
Bene (well)	**Meglio** (better)
Male (badly)	**Peggio** (worse)
Molto (much)	**Più** (more)
Poco (little)	**Meno** (less)

13.2 - The superlative

In Italian the superlative has two possible forms: **relative superlative** and **absolute superlative**.

13.2.1 - Relative superlative

Relative superlative expresses the highest or the least degree of a quality compared to that of other entities.

13.2.1.1 - Expressing the highest degree of a quality

To express the highest degree of a quality in Italian you use **an article** + **più** before an adjective and either the word **di** or the word **fra** before the second term of comparison.

The article that precedes the word **più** agrees with the first term of comparison.

Examples:

Luca è **il più** forte **della** classe
Luca is the strongest in the class

Lucia è **la più** simpatica **tra i** nostri amici

Lucia is the funniest amongst our friends

Since in the first example the first term of comparison is Luca, a male, the article to be used is the masculine singular *il*.

Since in the second example the first term of comparison is Lucia, a female, the article to be used is the feminine singular *la*.

13.2.1.2 - *Expressing the least degree of a quality*

To express the least degree of a quality in Italian, use **an article + meno** before an adjective, and either the word **di** or the word **fra** before the second term of comparison.

Also in this case, the article that precedes the word **meno** agrees with the first term of comparison.

Examples:

Luca e Giacomo sono **i meno** forti **della** classe

Luca and Giacomo are the least strong in the class

Lucia è **la meno** simpatica **tra i** nostri amici

Lucia is the least funny amongst our friends

13.2.2 - Absolute superlative

Absolute superlative expresses the highest degree of a quality without being compared to that of other entities.

13.2.2.1 - Expressing the highest degree of a quality

To express the highest degree of a quality, you just add **-issimo**, **-issima**, **-issimi**, or **-issime** to the adjective's base.

The adjective's base is formed by deleting the last vowel of an adjective.

For example, if the adjective is *elegante*, the adjective's base is *elegant*. If the adjective is *furbo*, the adjective's base is *furb*.

Examples:

Maria era elegantissima stasera
Maria was very elegant tonight

Giovanni e Riccardo erano elegantissimi stasera
Giovanni and Riccardo were very elegant tonight

13.2.3 - Other ways to form absolute superlative

In Italian there are at least two other ways to form absolute superlative.

FIRST ALTERNATIVE WAY

You can form absolute superlative also by placing one of these words before the adjective: *molto, assai, incredibilmente, estremamente*.

Examples:

a. Daniela è *molto* intelligente -> Daniela is very intelligent

b. Daniela è *assai* intelligente -> Daniela is very intelligent

c. Daniela è *incredibilmente* intelligente -> Daniela is incredibly intelligent

d. Daniela è *estremamente* intelligente -> Daniela is extremely intelligent

All the examples above are normally widely used in spoken Italian.

SECOND ALTERNATIVE WAY

You can form absolute superlative also by placing one of these words before the adjective – without leaving any space – *ultra, extra, stra, super, iper*.

Examples:

a. Ieri franco era *superfelice* -> Yesterday Franco was very happy
b. Ieri franco era *extrafelice* -> Yesterday Franco was very happy
c. Ieri franco era *ultrafelice* -> Yesterday Franco was very happy
d. Ieri franco era *strafelice* -> Yesterday Franco was very happy
e. Ieri franco era *iperfelice* -> Yesterday Franco was very happy

In spoken Italian the most common suffixes to form absolute superlative are: *stra*, *ultra*, *super*.

13.2.4 - Irregular superlative forms

In Italian there are also some superlatives that are formed irregularly. In the table below, you'll find the most common ones.

ADJECTIVE	RELATIVE SUPERLATIVE	TRANSLATION
Buono	Il migliore	The best
Cattivo	Il peggiore	The worst
Grande	Il maggiore	The biggest
Piccolo	Il minore	The smallest

ADJECTIVE	ABSOLUTE SUPERLATIVE	TRANSLATION
Buono	Buonissimo/Ottimo	Very good
Cattivo	Cattivissimo/Pessimo	Very bad
Grande	Grandissimo/Massimo	Very big
Piccolo	Piccolissimo/Minimo	Very small

Chapter 14
The impersonal form

The impersonal form takes place when verbs express an action without indicating who is the subject that's carrying out that action.

The impersonal form in Italian is usually used only at the 3rd person singular.

In Italian there can be both impersonal verbs and impersonal expressions.

All the followings can be impersonal in Italian:

- Verbs indicating meteorological phenomenons: *nevicare, piovere, grandinare, gelare, tuonare*, etc.

    Ex: Guarda! **Nevica**!
    Look! It's snowing!

- Expressions composed of fa + adjective/noun: *fa caldo, fa bello, fa freddo, fa brutto*, etc.

Ex: Oggi **fa** veramente **caldo**

It's really hot today

- Verb to be + adjective/adverb: *è possibile che, è assurdo che, è bene che*, etc.

  Ex: **E' possibile che** qualcuno l'abbia rubato

  It's possible someone stole it

- Verb to be + temporal expressions: : *è da settimane che, è da poco che, è una vita che*, etc.

  Ex: **E' da settimane che** non risponde al telefono

  It's been weeks that he's not picked up the phone

- Verbs such as: *sembrare, accadere, succedere, bisognare, bastare, parere*, etc.

  Ex: **Sembra** che si sia calmato

  It seems he has calmed down

- Some passive verbs indicating prohibitions or permissions: *è vietato, è proibito, è permesso, è concesso*, etc.

  Ex: **E' vietato** camminare sull'erba

It's forbidden to walk on the grass

- The expression si + verb

    Ex: **Si mangia** molto bene in Italia
    In Italy one eats very well

OTHER INFORMATION

When you want to form the impersonal form with compound tenses, you should always use the auxiliary "to be."

Ex: **E' bastato** un rimprovero per farlo smettere
It was enough of a reproach to make him stop

However, with verbs indicating meteorological phenomenons, you can use either the auxiliary "to have" or the auxiliary "to be."

Ex: **Ha nevicato/è nevicato**
It has snowed

14.1 – The impersonal form with si

One way to form impersonal sentences in Italian is by using the word si before a verb.

This construction can be used with both transitive and intransitive verbs, and, in both cases, si can be followed only by a verb in the third person singular.

Examples:

a. Di sera si gioca a carte
One plays cards in the evening/we play cards in the evening

b. Qui si studia molto
One studies a lot here/we study a lot here

As you can see, example "a" shows an intransitive verb since *giocare* doesn't require a direct object. Example "b" on the other hand, shows a transitive verb since *studiare* requires a direct object. Direct objects can be expressed or implied. In example "b" the direct object is implied. The same example can also be written with an expressed direct object: *Qui si studia molto matematica*, meaning "We study math a lot here."

IMPERSONAL FORM WITH SI WITH COMPOUND TENSES

When the impersonal form with **si** is used with compound tenses, the verbs that normally need the auxiliary "avere" need instead the *auxiliary essere*.

Ex 1: **Si** è parlato molto di te
We talked a lot about you

"Parlare" is a verb that requires the auxiliary "avere": *Abbiamo parlato molto di te*, meaning "We talked a lot about you."

However, as you can see from example 1, when "parlare" is used in compound tenses with the impersonal form with "si," it requires the auxiliary "essere."

Since the auxiliary "to be" used is *essere*, when the impersonal form with "si" is used with compound tenses of transitive verbs, the *past participle* always agrees in gender and number with the direct object (when this is expressed).

Ex 2: **Si** è *bevuta* molta birra alla festa
We drank a lot of beer at the party

In example 2 the direct object is "birra," a noun which is feminine singular in Italian. So, the past participle will end in -a, *bevuta*, since it agrees with the direct object.

IMPERSONAL FORM WITH SI WITH REFLEXIVE VERBS

The impersonal form with **si** can be used also with reflexive verbs.
In this case, reflexive verbs can be used only in the third person singular.

Pay attention because the third person singular of reflexive verbs will be **ci si** + verb, and not si si + verb.

Ex: **Ci si** veste leggere in estate
One dresses light in summer/We dress light in summer

Chapter 15
Conditional clauses

Conditional clauses – also called if sentences or hypothetical period – are a way to express a hypothesis.

Conditional clauses are composed of an *independent clause* – expressing a consequence – and a dependent clause – expressing a condition and usually beginning with one of the following words *se, nel caso che, qualora, a condizione che, posto che, nell'ipotesi che*, etc. In Italian, *se* is usually the most common word used to create conditional clauses.

The *independent clause* can precede or follow the dependent clause. The choice is up to you.

Examples:

- (subordinate) Se fai i capricci, (main) *non andremo in piscina*
If you keep throwing tantrums, we won't go to the pool
- (main) *Non andremo in piscina*, (subordinate) se fai i capricci
We won't go to the pool, if you keep throwing tantrums

So, if you keep throwing tantrums, the consequence will be that we won't go to the swimming pool.

Let's see how to create conditional clauses that express certainty.

15.1 – Conditional clauses expressing certainty

In these conditional clauses the speaker is sure – or there's a very high possibility – that the hypothesis/condition is fulfilled.

FORMATION

Se + present indicative, passato prossimo or future + dependent clause + present indicative, passato prossimo or future/imperative + independent clause

Examples:

a. Se piove, non andremo al lago (present + future)
If it rains, we won't go to the sea

b. Se piove, non andiamo al lago (present + present)
If it rains, we don't go to the sea

c. Se pioverà, non andremo al lago (future + future)

If it'll rain, we won't go to the sea

d. Se le hai mentito, hai sbagliato (p. prossimo + p. prossimo)

If you lied to her, you've made a mistake.

e. Se hai mangiato troppo, prendi un digestivo! (p. prossimo + imperative)

If you ate too much, take a digestive enzyme!

Glossary

Adjective

In general, an adjective is a word that describes a person or thing.

Adverb

An adverb is a word that adds more information to a verb, a noun, another adverb, an adjective or a phrase. Adverbs can be of place, time, cause, degree, manner, etc.

Auxiliary verb

An auxiliary verb is a verb used to form the tenses of other verbs.

Concession – Concessive clauses

A concessive clause is a clause that can signal a contrast, a qualification, or a concession in relation to the idea expressed in the main clause

Conjunction

A conjunction is a word that links together words, phrases, or sentences.

Modal verb

A modal verb is a verb that is used usually with another verb to express possibility, necessity, or permission.

Glossary

Adjective

In general, an adjective is a word that describes a person or thing.

Adverb

An adverb is a word that adds more information to a verb, a noun, another adverb, an adjective or a phrase. Adverbs can be of place, time, cause, degree, manner, etc.

Auxiliary verb

An auxiliary verb is a verb used to form the tenses of other verbs.

Concession – Concessive clauses

A concessive clause is a clause that can signal a contrast, a qualification, or a concession in relation to the idea expressed in the main clause

Conjunction

A conjunction is a word that links together words, phrases, or sentences.

Modal verb

A modal verb is a verb that is used usually with another verb to express possibility, necessity, or permission.

Noun

A noun is a word that identifies a person, thing, or place.

Preposition

A preposition is a word – sometimes a group of words (see contracted prepositions) – that is used before a noun or a pronoun to show position, place, time, manner, etc.

Pronoun

A pronoun is a word that replaces a noun.

Verb

A verb is a word – or a group of words – that expresses a state, an action, or an experience.

Contacts

You can contact me by email, by clicking the page *Contact me* on my website **sositalian.com**

Printed by Amazon Italia Logistica S.r.l.
Torrazza Piemonte (TO), Italy